SUCCESSFUL
GOOSE
HUNTING

SUCCESSFUL GOOSE HUNTING

Charles L. Cadieux

Stone Wall Press, Inc.
1241 30th St., N.W.
Washington, D.C. 20007

Library of Congress Catalog Card Number 86-081733
Cadieux, Charles L.
Successful Goose Hunting

ISBN 0-913276-52-9

Copyright © 1986 by Stone Wall Press Inc.
1241 30th Street, NW-Washington, D.C.

Printed in the United States of America

Table of Contents

Chapter 1

Description of North American Geese

A few miles out of Easton, Maryland, a flock of geese talk excitedly as they get ready to go out for the morning feeding. They take wing heavily, with a bit of "walking on the water" thrown in to help them get airborne. They circle away from land, out over the Chesapeake Bay, to gain altitude. These are veteran birds; they've been shot at several times enroute from their Canadian breeding grounds, and once or twice since they reached their winter home on Maryland's Eastern Shore.

Two hundred yards above the cut-over cornfields, the big birds turn east into the rays of the November sun. From their vantage point they can see four groups of decoys in the fields ahead of them. They fly steadily on, heading farther east. The decoys have become all too familiar to them as they worked their way south to this wintering area. Decoys alone seem to have no pulling effect this morning. But one group of decoys is different; it talks to the flying geese in their own language. Crouched in a spacious pit blind, Francis Howard held a goose call to his lips and sent out beautiful music—talking to those geese, explaining that there was lots of shelled corn left on the ground, plus a few green sprouts that would make a fine breakfast. In the other end of the blind son Steve used his call with equal effect. I was the lucky guy in the middle. With those two blowing calls, mine remained in my pocket. Longtime Easton resident, Francis operates the Tideland Sporting Goods and lives goose hunting and goose hunters for five months of every year.

The geese swung to the expert calls, hurrying to join their friends in a safe feeding area. They swung past the decoys, heads down and eyes searching for some flaw in the set-up. A few very quiet calls came from the two experts, the sounds of feeding geese. Turning into final approach pattern, they lowered flaps and bucketed air with big wings as their black feet stretched toward the ground.

The lead bird had almost touched down when Francis said, "Take 'em!" He threw back the chicken wire and camouflage cloth lid to our blind and the three of us came up with shotguns ready. I carefully picked one, two, three birds out of the flock which were fighting for altitude. Without looking around I knew that the other two had scored three clean hits each. They could hardly miss at this close range.

We were done for the day; so we spent some time congratulating ourselves on our good fortune and admiring the birds as the retriever brought them to hand.

These were Canadas, intermediate in size, averaging about five pounds in weight. They were handsome birds, sporting the typical Canadian color scheme: black heads with bright white cheek patches, black necks, soft gray breasts and back, striped and flecked with indistinct darker lines. A white area on the forward half of the tail contrasted sharply with the shiny black tail feathers. Their feet and legs were dark black. This was successful goose hunting.

*   *   *

We are lying on our sides, propped up on one elbow, and we are wearing chest waders, for the plowing is soft and squishy mud—mud which clings to our feet and balls up so that it is difficult to walk. But we don't have to walk. About three hundred white paper napkins in front of us are blowing gently in the wind, each one of them rubber-banded to the top of a willowy stake. Interspersed with the paper napkins, another two dozen full-bodied white goose decoys stand with heads erect, trying to lend a genuine appearance to a fake set up.

There are thousands of geese on the Lissie Prairie here in Texas, and half of them are in the air, trading back and forth, talking up a storm. They run about 80% white geese, 15% blue phase snows, and the other 5% a surprising population of whitefronts. Geese are in flight within our sight for two hours, but nothing comes our way. The three of us lie still and discuss the situation in quiet tones, although no goose could hear us over the din they were making.

By 9:30 A.M. not a shot had been fired, even though the steady drumroll of shooting from half a mile to the north of us was making us green with envy. By 9:45 a strong breeze had sprung up. My host got up and pulled out a kite shaped roughly like a snow goose. He quickly streamed it in the freshening breeze, then got back in his damp hidey-hole. "Be ready," he said, "it works every time."

Fifteen minutes went by while we watched the kite tack back and forth over our decoy spread. Then Roubideaux went "Psssst! Mark west!" I swiveled around in time to see a hundred snows swinging right

into our deeks. Two shots were fired before I got to my cold-stiffened knees and was ready to fire. I still had time to knock two white birds out of the sky. The limit was five in those days, and half an hour later we attracted another flock right into the deeks and wreaked havoc among them. As the black Lab sloshed busily through the mud, the pile of white birds grew to fourteen. The dog stopped work and looked at us with an expression calling for compliments. After he got the compliments Roubideaux sent him out again and hand-signalled him onto an immature blue that he had seen come scaling down two city blocks away. All of our birds (except that one immature blue phase) were all white with black wing tips, and with the characteristic rust colored tinting around the head and neck, and with pink feet. Again, this was successful goose hunting.

*   *   *

Albemarle Sound, North Carolina, and we are freezing in a floating torture pen known as a sink box. It is flush with the water level, and I'm trying to avoid the wind-blown spray by hiding my head behind the full-bodied snow goose decoy that is perched on one corner of the box. Grey, scudding clouds greeted us when we were ferried out that morning, and the wet wind was reason enough to wish that I had not yielded to the beckoning aroma of hot coffee and sausages that morning. I should have stayed in bed—the geese sure did. By the time the sun burned the low-lying clouds away and began to warm my bones, it was 10:30. So far it had been a day to forget quickly.

The warm sun lulled me into drowsiness, but not my guide. The lanky Tarheel murmured, "Mark southeast."

A thin wavering line of white birds were stringing across the sky, headed for some destination far to the west. Going to the mainland, I surmised. I slid my call into action and began working on them. It wasn't the fault of the call—made for me by the virtuoso of goose calls, Frankie Heidelbauer, two years after he won the world's goose calling championship with a similar call in 1953 and 1954. But these white birds—all of them the familiar white with black wing tips—paid no heed to my pleadings and disappeared into the western distances.

The wind had died, and the sun was warm. We broke out coffee and sandwiches—sandwiches made of sliced goose breast and lots of homemade butter on home made bread. We were so busy eating that we didn't seen the birds until they were almost upon us. A long string of white geese! Both the guide and I began our wheedling yelps on the calls, and this time that was the only invitation the birds needed. "Don't call while they're coming closer," said my guide, and I slid the call down out of sight and kept my face down to avoid any sunlight reflection from my eyeglasses.

"Now!" barked the guide and we came struggling up to our knees. Swinging awkwardly, I centered a white goose and dropped it. A second target shed a puff of feathers, then folded up with my third shot and came splashing down some fifty yards from the sink box.

This was definitely successful goose hunting. No blue phase birds were in this flock of snow geese, for these were the Greater Snow Geese, native to the eastern fourth of the continent and not found out west at all. Pink beaks and pink feet and black primaries on the wings—everything else was snow white. This Greater Snow Goose weighs in at an average of six pounds, with exceptional specimens going seven and one half.

* * *

Obviously, there are many kinds of geese and many ways to hunt them. A farmer's son carrying the shotgun on the tractor with him suddenly stops the machine, slides off the far side and gets down on his belly on the North Dakota stubble. He crawls to within shooting range and drops two big honkers—they weigh in about 14 pounds each!

In Western Nebraska, I shot the smallest snow goose I'd ever seen. Turns out it wasn't a snow goose at all, but a Ross's Goose—a bird we didn't even know existed some fifty years ago. For no one had noticed these runts in the lesser snow goose flock before that time. Beautiful little bird, smaller than some mallard drakes, he most definitely was a goose.

So let's figure it out. How many species of geese are there in North America?

Canadas

Branta Canadensis, is the dark Canadian goose, the one we identify by its black head and neck with the snow white cheek patch, black feet and beak. They range in size from under two pounds to nearly twenty pounds. But they are all Canada geese!

13

This goose statue at Wawa, Ontario, honors all of the subspecies. "Wawa" is an Indian word describing the call of the wild goose.

Most of the taxonomists now agree that there are eleven races of *Branta canadensis,* These eleven subspecies are:

1. *Branta canadensis canadensis,* the Atlantic Canada Goose.
2. *Branta canadensis interior,* Hudson Bay Canada Goose.
3. *Branta canadensis maxima,* Giant Canada Goose.
4. *Branta canadensis moffitti,* Great Basin Canada Goose.
5. *Branta canadensis parvipes,* Lesser Canada Goose.
6. *Branta canadensis taverneri,* Alaskan Canada Goose.
7. *Branta canadensis fulva,* Vancouver Canada Goose.
8. *Branta canadensis occidentalis,* Dusky Canada Goose.
9. *Branta canadensis leucopareia,* Aleutian Goose.
10. *Branta canadensis minima,* Cackling Canada Goose.
11. *Branta canadensis hutchinsii,* Richardson Canada Goose.

Branta canadensis maxima is the largest of them all. This big fellow was fairly common in the northern Great Plains and western portion of the Mississippi Flyway back in the days when the frontier was slowly moving west. Naturally, they were the most sought after and heavily gunned. Famous hunter-writer Ray Holland told of geese weigh-

A splendid example of a "maxima" Canada goose.

ing 20 pounds, shot on the North Dakota prairie. One report says that G.M. Hogue shot a 23 pounder from Steele County, North Dakota in 1909. Well-known goose authority from my home town of Jamestown, North Dakota, Carl Strutz has weighed specimens to twenty pounds, but his were captive, and captives might be fatter than wild birds. Morton Barrows reported a 24 pounder from Heron Lake, Minnesota in 1900. But these were too old to be believed, until along came an 18¾ pounder from near Oakes, North Dakota in 1947.

Just when we thought they were gone, in 1962 we realized that we had some huge birds wintering at the Mayo Brothers Clinic town of Rochester, Minnesota. These were the descendants of geese purchased by Dr. Charles Mayo in the 1920's and released into the environs of Rochester. The municipal power plant provided the warm water which stayed open all year.

At the invitation of Minnesota authorities, Harold Hansen weighed and measured birds captured from the flock which wintered there. The results told him that he was looking at the long gone "maximas". The same Harold Hansen has written a book about the Giant Canadas which is recommended reading to anyone interested in these "biggest of them all" Canada geese. Given protection and helped by some transplanting efforts, the *maxima* has made a satisfying recovery. One of the latest efforts to spread his range was the introduction of captive nesters to the Audubon National Wildlife Refuge on the Snake Creek Arm of Garrison Reservoir in North Dakota. Here the birds have had excellent nesting success, using the raised platforms provided for them over water. Juvenile survival has been good and there are high hopes for these birds. The pre-white man settlement range of the giant Canada included Missouri, Kansas, Illinois, Indiana, the northwest corner of Ohio, and north through Minnesota and the Dakotas to the southern halves of Alberta, Manitoba and Saskatchewan.

In Missouri, captive breeders of *maxima* have been productive. But the birds have become too tame and refuse to migrate. In fact, they refuse to leave the front yards of many lakeside residences. Attempts to open a hunting season were met with opposition by the lakesiders who enjoy having the decorative and overly-friendly birds on their front lawns. But the big birds in Missouri have not lost their native caution. When the hunting season opened, a few were dropped before they got the idea; then they became quite wary and suspicious. Joel Vance,

The maximas are the largest subspecies of Canada, and are now being widely distributed as ancient coverts are being restocked.

knowledgeable waterfowler with the Missouri Department of Conservation, tells me that:

"We do hunt our geese and they are far from pets. The flap at Lake Taneycomo was a tempest in a teapot. The people down there had fed the birds and made them into scenic pests. About half the residents wanted them around to look at; the rest were tired of wading in goose droppings and having their gardens and lawns munched.

We compromised and established a 'no fire' zone, but allowed hunting outside of that. No bloodbath ensued. The birds got smart and wild almost instantly, and the hunt was a good one. These Giant Canadas are smart birds."

Missouri has done an excellent job of trapping and transplanting the increase from their "maxima" flock, which now numbers about 11,000 of these giants in Missouri. Not all of these giant Canadas are the result of transplanting, far from it. Missouri has always had a family of *maximas* nesting in the cliffs along the Missouri River. These birds are still there and prospering.

Rochester, Minnesota is host to about 20,000 of the giant birds. The Rochester birds are smart enough to be tame where they cannot be shot at (in the city itself), but also smart enough to be very much wilder in the countryside where they range for food. They are simply intelligent enough to take advantage of a good thing when they see it.

There are certainly more than 180,000 of these "giant Canadas" today, and the prognosis looks good for more.

There's a great population of Canadas called *Branta canadensis hutchinsii*, known popularly as Hutchins, or simply "hutch's". These birds nest on the Shortgrass prairie all the way northward to the MacKenzie Delta of Canada, south into Alberta and Saskatchewan, and migrate southward through southeastern Colorado to winter on the Washita National Wildlife Refuge and at Buffalo Lake and Muleshoe National Wildlife Refuges. A few formerly wintered in northeastern New Mexico, but those birds seem to have been shortstopped along the front range of Colorado.

They weigh in at three pounds each, on average, and are delectable on the table. Like all wild geese, they are athletes and lack the fat which makes the domestic goose unpalatable to many.

There's another small race of Canadas named *Branta canadensis leucopareia*, which had a narrow brush with extinction. These Aleutian geese nested only on a few islands in the fog-shrouded, cold, wet and windy Aleutian Islands. Before Seward wrapped up the best real estate deal in all history, some Russians tried fur-farming foxes, the easy way. Just turn them loose on an uninhabited island and let them forage for themselves. It worked well for the fur dealers, but it wreaked havoc among the resident wildlife which had evolved without any predators being around to worry about. When Americans took over the mismanagement of the priceless resources of the Aleutians, they continued the fox-farming bit, because it was profitable.

By the time somebody listened to the warnings of the biologists, the Aleutian goose was almost a goner. The island of Agattu offers a case history. Prior to 1922, there were no foxes on Agattu and the Aleutian goose bred there by the thousands. In 1923 four Arctic foxes were released there, and another 5 in 1924. Another 23 Arctic foxes were released in 1930. More than a thousand foxes were killed for their

The Aleutian subspecies of Canada goose.

pelts by the year 1950. The foxes had prospered because of the abundant local food supply. Part of that food supply was the ground-nesting Aleutian goose. For practical purposes the Aleutian goose was exterminated from Agattu by the year 1937! By 1962, the only known nesting population of Aleutian geese was on Buldir Island, where the fox had never been introduced.

In 1963, I went from Albuquerque up to Monte Vista NWR in Colorado to photograph Aleutian goslings which had been trapped on Buldir and brought to the refuge for rearing. A captive flock was built up and transferred to Patuxent, Maryland where they got the attention of the Fish and Wildlife Service's best aviculturists.

Then the Fish and Wildlife Service went to work on the problem of the Arctic foxes, which **were never native** to the Aleutian Islands. They used the species-selective Compound 1080 to remove all of the foxes on Amchitka, on Agattu, and on other Aleutian Islands deemed suited to hosting these small Canadas.

The Patuxent production line was in full swing and the Service was able to restock hundreds of Aleutian geese back into the Aleutians. At first it was thought that the restocking was in vain, but—finally—a few Aleutian birds, marked with the Service's identifying bands, showed up on California wintering grounds. The status of these birds today is best summed up as still endangered but showing promise. For more information on this endangered subspecies, please see my book, THESE ARE THE ENDANGERED, which is available from Stone Wall Press.

Branta canadensis fulva, the Vancouver Canada goose, sometimes doesn't bother to migrate. It finds all it needs in the central part of southern British Columbia, where favorable ocean currents allow Victoria gardeners to grow roses in January. The entire family of Canadas shows a growing reluctance to migrate! If they can find what they want farther north, they'll winter farther north.

There are other strains of Canada goose which we will talk about later, but for right now, we can say that Canada geese range in weight from 2½ to 21 pounds, with most "families" ranging in the median five to nine pound range. If it is colored like a Canada; it's a Canada. And speaking for the wonderful family of Canada geese, from 2½ pounds to 21 pounders, their resurgence in numbers is one of the greatest successes of modern waterfowl management. In all, they probably number about 3¾ million.

Wintering grounds on the Atlantic and Mississippi Flyways are probably holding more Canada geese right now than they should be holding. The world's best goose hunting over a large area—year in and year out—is on the Eastern Shore of Chesapeake Bay. But more and more Canadas are wintering north of there, and that poses the problems of too much familiarity with men. At the same time, the southern end of the flyways—Florida in the Atlantic and Louisiana in the Mississippi—could surely be wintering home to many more Canadas than they now support. But figure out how to accomplish this, will you please?

Denver boasts a resident "golf course" population of Canadas, but the wintering population in central and southern New Mexico has shrunk to the point of almost disappearing. We have no problems in **numbers** of Canada geese; we do have problems with distribution!

Goose management biologists speak of discrete *populations* of Canadas, a classification which is based solely on the fact that they

These free-flying Canadas are residents in Denver's parks and golf courses.

21

occupy identifiable nesting grounds, migrate along identifiable migration paths, and winter in identifiable areas.

This "population" classification system speaks of twelve different populations:

1. North Atlantic Population
2. Mid-Atlantic Population
3. Tennessee Valley Population
4. Mississippi Valley Population
5. Eastern Prairie Population
6. Western Prairie Population
7. Tall Grass Prairie Population
8. Short Grass Prairie Population
9. Highline Population
10. Intermountain Population
11. Northwest Coastal Population
12. Alaskan Population

The North Atlantic Population is composed almost entirely of *Branta canadensis canadensis* subspecies. They nest across Newfoundland and Labrador, migrate southward along the Atlantic Coast, seldom venture very far inland, and winter in many isolated groups from Newfoundland itself all the way south to the sunny shores of Pea Island National Wildlife Refuge in North Carolina. Formerly, this family went all the way south to Florida and the Gulf Coast to winter—but no more.

The Mid-Atlantic Population is the largest segment of wintering Canada geese. The great majority of them are of the subspecies *Branta canadensis interior*, but there are as many as 18,000 of the Giant strain, which migrates from Ohio over to the Chesapeake Bay area to spend the winter. The "Interior" strain nests from the Ungava Peninsula all the way across to Hudson and James Bay, northward through all of the wet tundra areas of central and eastern Canada. Most of them winter in the Delmarva Peninsula area of the East Coast. These are the birds that darken the skies from Chestertown, Maryland south to the Norfolk Bay Bridge, and from the Eastern Shore across to Ocean City.

The Tennessee Valley Population, made up of some giant strain "maximas" and a lot of "interior" birds, is an example of the changes man has wrought in the wintering distribution of Canada geese. Originally, this population traces its beginnings to Wheeler National Wildlife Refuge in Alabama. Here a captive flock was started to remedy the deplorable situation wherein Alabama sported as few as 600 Canada geese in their wintering flock. Boy oh boy, have they increased and multiplied! This population nests southeast of Hudson Bay north to Akimiski Island. They winter from southern Ontario and Michigan, all the way down to Tennessee and Alabama.

The Mississippi Valley population, composed of 95% *Branta canadensis interior* plus a handful of "maximas", nests west of James Bay and south of Hudson Bay and migrates south through Minnesota, Wisconsin. These geese winter in southern Illinois and adjacent Kentucky. There are now as many as 350,000 to 500,000 wintering in this great flock.

The Eastern Prairie Population, *B.c. interior* plus some 30,000 maximas, nests in a big area north from the Machichi River, 20 miles east of York Factory to 80 miles north of Churchill, from Lake Winnipeg northeast to Hudson Bay. The maxima part of this population migrates to Minnesota and spend the winter in and near to Rochester,

Canada geese are strong fliers. These birds are alighting on water after a migration flight.

where they have the famed Mayo Brothers to take care of their health problems, should any develop. The more numerous "interiors" migrate southeastward and winter on or near to Swan Lake National Wildlife Refuge in Missouri.

The Western Prairie Population, a small one, is composed of "interiors" with a scattering of the "often-transplanted" Maximas. They nest north of Dauphin, Manitoba and Yorkton, Saskatchewan. They migrate south to meet the Missouri River near Bismarck, North Dakota and then follow the river down to Lake Andes, South Dakota, where a large portion of them winter. Others go on to Squaw Creek National Wildlife Refuge in Missouri. A few continue on down to the Gambell Refuge near Paris, Texas.

The Short Grass Prairie Population, is made up of 90% *B.c. parvipes*, the so-called "lesser" Canada. The other ten percent are half "hutch's" and half "moffitti", the Great Basin Canada Goose. Their nesting area is spread across a huge chunk of Canada from Victoria Island across to the MacKenzie Delta, south into the northern part of both Alberta and Saskatchewan. These are the birds which winter in southeastern Colorado, across to the Washita, Buffalo Lake and Muleshoe National Wildlife Refuges. A few of them reach the northeastern corner of New Mexico, but very few, for the front range flock of Colorado's fat and happy honkers have effectively shortstopped their migration and they no longer reach New Mexico.

The Highline Population includes some of the maximas and lots of the moffittii. These birds nest from the Cypress Hills across the plains region of Alberta, and down into eastern Montana and Wyoming—east of the Rockies. Some few of them reach wintering grounds at the Las Vegas-Maxwell National Wildlife Refuges in New Mexico, and some of them stay north on the North Platte River in southeastern Wyoming. But the great majority of them now winter in eastern Colorado. A significant part of this population previously went on south to the Bosque del Apache NWR in New Mexico, but no more. Today, that refuge is working with a resident population of nesting birds, hoping to reestablish its wintering population.

The Intermountain population are all "great basin" gesse, which nest in central British Columbia east to central Alberta, along the Chilcotin and Cariboo plateaus, into the Flathead valley of Montana and the Upper Green River in Wyoming, and even down to the Carson Sink in Nevada. They winter from the Columbia Basin in Washington and Oregon, the Harney Basin in Oregon, the Snake River Plain in Idaho and down into the Central and Imperial Valleys of California.

The Northwest Coastal Population consists of *B.c. occidentalis*, the so-called dusky Canada, plus some *B.c. fulva*, The Vancouver Canada Goose. This "population" seems to me to be a very arbitrary one, without real reason for existence. The dusky Canadas find their favorite nesting grounds centered on Cordova, Alaska, while the Vancouver Canadas nest as far south as southern Vancouver Island, and some of the Vancouvers aren't even migratory. We therefore cannot assign them the same wintering grounds with the duskies. However, for purposes of this discussion, the Northwest Coastal Population is defined as nesting between Cook Inlet and Bering Glacier in Alaska, also the Queen Charlotte Island, Vancouver Island and the Alexander archipelago in Alaska. Those that do migrate (most of them) winter in the Willamette Valley of Oregon, and in Benton, Lane and Polk Counties of Oregon.

The Alaskan Population of Canadas comprises three subspecies— the cackling, Taverner (Alaskan) and Aleutian. They nest over most of

Fellow members of waterfowl aristocracy, a Canada goose of the Great Basin population poses with mallard drakes.

Alaska, from the Aleutians to the high tundra south of the Brooks Range. The very important Yukon Delta has more than 200,000 nesters in good years, and these are cacklers. Remember that when you hear of plans to dam up the Yukon. It could be fatal to this huge population of geese.

These birds winter in interior Washington State, in northeastern Oregon and down in the Central Valley of California, as well as in the San Francisco Bay area.

This completes our taxonomic discussion of the great family of Canada geese. They are arranged in eleven subspecies and twelve discrete populations. Some are bigger than others, but all are Canadas, the king of waterfowl.

Greater Snow Goose

This white goose with black wing tips is not a small bird. No indeed! The greater snow goose averages around six and one half pounds. They nest farther north than any other goose, with most of the nesting grounds in the Canadian Arctic and in Greenland. They are colony nesters, and thousands of pairs will be incubating eggs within sight of each other. Arctic foxes take a terrific toll of the defenseless ground nesters, but their system of nesting in one huge colony seems to work, for their numbers are increasing yearly. However, the nesting season is very short this far north, and a single catastrophic storm can, and has, wiped out an entire year's production. We are seeing the results of several good nesting seasons one after the other as this book goes to press.

Fifty years ago this big white goose of the eastern seaboard was in trouble. Heavily hunted on its wintering grounds, it suffered a few years of catastrophic weather in the far northern reaches of Canada where it nests—and its numbers plummeted to less than ten thousand.

Acting more swiftly than usual, the federal government closed the hunting season on greater snow geese on the Atlantic Coast. (They are not found in the western three flyways.) The feds decided to bring the greater snow goose up to a population of 100,000 and then keep it there. Litigation from wildlife interests that wanted the resurgence to continue held up implementation of those regulations and the greater

Greater snow geese, photographed near Pea Island NWR in North Carolina.

snow goose population went right on past the 100,000 signpost and hit 150,000 before the feds could get the season opened.

Hunting didn't seem to stop the increase, and there are nearly 300,000 greater snow geese wintering along the Atlantic seaboard from the Carolinas north through New Jersey. Too few are being killed now—and the flocks are at dangerous high levels. The main reason for the great improvement in census figures is the existence of wildlife refuges that were simply not there fifty years ago when the population took such a beating.

We've got a problem now with the greater snow goose. Simply stated, we have too many for the wintering grounds to carry without damaging the habitat and we are killing far too few. The amount of salt grass habitat left on the Atlantic Coast is surprisingly small—outside of the refuges. Because refuges concentrate the birds in huge flocks, and feed those birds to keep them on the refuges, the kill is small. There is a temptation to say, "Hurrah, we've got too many!", but the prognosis is that increasing number of birds in decreasing acres of habitat will surely lead to a disease solution of the problem.

As of now, we have too many greater snow geese.

Lesser Snow Goose

The "lesser" snow goose weighs in at one pound less than the Greater Snow Goose, but he is far more numerous. At the present time, there are at least two and one half million of the blue and snow geese we lump together as Lesser Snow Geese. The Central Flyway holds the most, more than a million, with the Mississippi Flyway just under a million and the Pacific Flyway holding about 400,000.

These slightly smaller snow geese nest a bit farther south than the bigger snow, but it is still Arctic with a very short nesting season. The greatest numbers of this "goose from beyond the north wind" nest along the Arctic Ocean shores of Canada, and on Victoria and Banks Islands.

This beautiful pair of snow and blue geese were photographed in flight by Judd Cooney. Different color phases, they were once thought to be separate species.

Ross's Goose

Smallest of all North American geese, the Ross's Goose is so little and so inconspicuous that it's existence was a secret until recently. About the same size, or smaller, than a good mallard drake, this all white goose is easily distinguished from the much larger snow goose when in the hand, but hard to see when flying in a gang of lesser snow geese.

The Ross's is entirely white; the snow goose has black wing tips. The snow goose has a darker colored "grinning patch" at the side of the beak; the Ross's does not. Evidently the littlest goose had nothing to grin about as he made his way up the evolutionary ladder.

They are colony nesters, and most of their young are hatched near McLaughlin Bay, 100 miles east of Perry River. Because they usually choose slightly elevated areas—not tidal marshes—in which to nest, they are somewhat protected from the rigors of the climate way up north.

Almost all of this uncommon species winter in the interior valleys of California, and it is postulated that these birds are from the biggest

The Ross's goose, smallest of the white geese, was photographed by Charles L. Cadieux.

nesting area, the one near McLaughlin Bay. But some birds are seen each year on migration paths that take them to Texas and Louisiana. No one knows for sure, but it is probable that these birds nest with, and migrate with, lesser snow geese from the McConnell River and Southhampton Island, where the nesting range of Ross's and snow goose overlaps. I've shot only one Ross's goose in my life, and that one was in Nebraska. Unless their numbers increase greatly, I don't really want to shoot another! Most of the Ross goose hunter mortality is caused by hunters who seek the snow goose. Because it is the smaller, it is seldom selected out of a flock of snows, which probably accounts for its relatively low hunter mortality.

No one has reported any sign of the color dimorphism which characterizes its kinfolk, the lesser snow goose.

Whitefronted Goose

This is the best eating of all the geese. Sorry, fellows, he is seldom found east of the Mississippi River. A true westerner, the two subspecies of whitefront live their lives on the unobstructed areas of western North America. They nest on the tundra, where they can see for miles in any direction, and they choose open prairie rest stops in migration, and winter on flat areas, without trees.

White front? Well, the forehead of this beautiful goose is white. The adults are very dark in appearance, sporting dark belly bands which give them the nickname of "tiger stripes" in some areas. They have bright orange feet, which helps in identification. The whitefront is circumpolar in distribution, but the Greenland nesters usually migrate to Europe, so we will concern ourselves only with the birds which nest across the northern tundra from Alaska to King William Island.

The more common subspecies, the Pacific whitefront, weighs in at 5 to 7 pounds, but there is a larger subspecies, the "Tule" subspecies which reaches slightly more than eight pounds when adult.

The Pacific whitefront winters on inland refuges in California, and on the coastal marshes of Texas and Louisiana and on down into Mexico where it can be found on the coastal marshes of Tampico and near Soto La Marina.

Bob Bry holds a fine specimen of whitefronted goose, killed on the prairies of North Dakota. This bird is seldom seen east of the Mississippi.

The larger "Tule" version winters almost exclusively in Butte, Colusa and Sutter Counties in California. In addition to the greater size, the Tule Whitefront is distinguished by having darker colors on the back and neck than the Pacific subspecies.

Biologists have found that the hatching rate of both these subspecies is very high, yet they have never filled the available habitat with breeding pairs. Why? Well, there's only a maximum of 120 days to get it all done—to fly in, select territories, build nests, lay eggs, incubate them for 22 days, rear the goslings, learn to fly and get headed south by the time the first hard frosts come, which is mid-August over much of their nesting area.

This excellent table bird deports himself in much the same manner as the mid-size Canadas. He decoys readily, until he gets farther south. By that time he has learned that decoys often make large noises and that some of this buddies seem to be missing after the loud noises. I found whitefronts in Old Mexico to be more sophisticated and careful than the much more numerous snow geese.

Calling a whitefront is a different matter from calling the other species. His "toodling" call is a high pitched sound, often described as "leek-leek"—repeated over and over. Once heard, it is never forgotten. But it is not easy to mimic.

If you live where whitefronts can be hunted, it will be worth your while to invest in some whitefront deeks and to learn to imitate its call. I'll take a whitefront over a similar sized Canada any day.

Emperor Goose

My friend Chris Batin, who lives in Fairbanks, Alaska, and edits a fine magazine known as Alaska Outdoors, will give us a detailed rundown of Alaska goosehunting in Chapter 13. Because I've not hunted either the Emperor, nor the Barnacle goose, I'll give just a short description of each bird and wait until Chris fills in our understanding of this fine pair of geese.

The Emperor is a smallish goose, limited to Alaska and Siberia in distribution. It has a white head and the back half of the neck is also white. Overall color is blue gray. The feet are orange or yellow.

The Emperor nests along the coast of Alaska from Kotzebue So-pund all the way down to the Aleutians. The Alaskan climate holds no terrors for the Emperor, and it winters in the Aleutians, which is "way down south" for this northerner.

Barnacle Goose

The Barnacle Goose is exceedingly rare with probably only about 40,000 in existence throughout the entire world. The occasional strag-gler has been reported on the Atlantic Coast, thought to be from the Greenland population, which usually migrates southeastward to Europe. I photographed these beautiful birds in Norway, but they are not seen in the Lower 48. They are my nomination for the most strikingly marked of all geese. Where the Canada family has a cheek patch, you would have to say that the Barnacle has a white face—not just the cheek. The underbelly is a snowy white in adults, and the back is strikingly barred in black and white. Although we don't see them, they are far from scarce, nesting almost around the North Pole—circumpo-

The barnacle goose, an important game species in Europe, nests in polar regions from Greenland to northern Siberia. Photographed in Norway by Chuck Cadieux.

lar is the word. There is a very large group in Greenland for the summer season, migrating to Scandinavia, Ireland and the shores of Merrie Old England to spend the winter.

In size they resemble the lesser snow goose, and they are equally acrobatic in flight. The Greenland families often nest on rocky shelves, high on a cliff. How do the babies get down to the water after hatching? Just like wood ducks falling out of a nesting box. They fall most of the way, bouncing off of rocks like little downy ping pong balls. Some of them do not survive the fall, but the majority do. I once saw cinematic proof that a day-old Barnacle gosling fell more than 300 feet, bounced off a solid rock point, fell another 150 feet and landed on rock. It then got up, shook itself and followed its concerned mother climbing over automobile-sized rocks enroute to the meadow. There the little goslings walked through grass and weeds for half a mile to reach the comparative safety of the water. Any bird that tough earns my undying admiration.

Nene Goose

Probably no sportsman will ever shoot a Nene goose (*Branta sandvicensis*). These beautiful birds are the state bird of Hawaii, but they are definitely not prospering there. Although it is a distant cousin of the Canada goose, the nene is very distinctive. Long adaptation to dry lava beds instead of wetlands has caused the nene to lose some of the webbing between its toes. It stands very erect, with proportionately longer legs than a Canada. It is about two feet tall, and measures roughly two feet from tip of beak to tail.

Exceedingly trustful, the Nene evolved in an Island paradise without meat-eating mammals besides man—and man seemed to let them alone until the white man came to louse up the idyllic heaven that was primitive Hawaii. The Nene was probably extinct on Maui by 1890, but a wild population persisted—and persists—on Hawaii. The wild population probably reached a low of less than 50 in 1952. The wild population has been supported by releases of pen-raised birds but has not shown an ability to maintain itself in the wild. Only a small percentage of Nenes breed each year. The average is only two goslings hatched per nesting pair, and losses to predators, against which the Nene has no

Two Nene geese, Hawaii's state bird, photographed in captivity.

escape mechanism, are very high. Introduced dogs, cats, mongooses, and feral pigs, all feed on the flightless young, and decimate the population of adults during the long molting period, when even the adults are flightless.

Introduced dogs and cats wreaked havoc with the trusting Nene, and his numbers are now definitely low. They presently exist in the wild only on Maui and the Big Island, Hawaii. The Department of Land and Natural Resources (in 1980) estimated that only 125 existed on Maui and perhaps 300 on Hawaii, despite a thirty year program of propagating the birds in captivity and releasing them into the wild. That 1980 estimate of 425 was a drastic decrease from the 1975 estimate of 875.

The National Park Service is cooperating with the Hawaii Department and the U.S. Fish and Wildlife Service in providing "predator resistant" enclosures in which wing clipped adults are breeding, with the hope that their young will populate surrounding territory. Starting in 1949, the Severn Wildfowl Trust in England began artificial propagation of the Nene and at the same time, Hawaii provided pairs to zoos which had no problem in rearing large numbers of Nene in captivity.

Litchfield, Connecticut is the site of a Nene propagation effort. Here, S. Dillon Ripley, famed Sectary Emeritus of the Smithsonian Institution has developed a flock of Nenes which numbered more than forty in late 1986. His seed stock came from Sir Peter Scott, the well-known English waterfowl expert. Ripley and Scott have cooperated in this Nene propagation effort since 1958, and have worked closely with Hawaiian authorities and with Hawaiian rancher Herbert C. Shipman. Ripley gives credit to Shipman as being the one man who has done the most to save the Nene from extinction. Shipman began his work in 1918, seven years after the hunting season had been officially closed on the Nene goose. Although he had troubles with the exotic mongoose, he did succeed in establishing a captive flock, which then provided the nucleus of breeding populations at the Mokapu Game Farm on Oahu. The fates have not been kind to the Nene. Even a tidal wave has been counted among their enemies. . . . a *tsunami* destroyed all but eleven of Shipman's Nenes in 1946.

The Nene has not succeeded in establishing itself in the wild, despite many re-introductions. It has been reared successfully in captivity and the captive population is growing in zoos and zoological parks and gardens around the world.

In 1965, it seemed the war against extinction had been won, and wild birds were seen in increasing numbers. Nevertheless, the same enemies—imported predators, domestic dogs and cats and constantly shrinking habitat—still stalk the Nene goose. Its position in the wild is now very precarious.

Certainly the future looks dark for the wild population of this lovely goose—an accident of evolution, which evolved where it did not need to be wary or cautious. When its world turned topsy-turvy with the arrival of white men and their animals, the Nene has not been able to cope.

Chapter 2

Great Goosehunting Spots

In the long and fascinating history of goose hunting in North America there are places where the goose hunting was so good that it defied description, places where the old timers found it easy to shoot a terrific number of geese in one day, where the market hunters flourished, where the supply of geese seemed endless.

Some of these places were always good—good when Columbus thought he'd landed on the shores of Asia, stayed good through the market hunting era, and perhaps are still good. Other places, where the hunting might have been just as fabulous, burned out after a bit. Others were creations of weird weather or changing farming practices. Their stories are but a brief spurt into immortality—a temporary bonanza. But all of these fabulous places provided fabulous hunting—the material from which great goose hunting tales are built.

Mattamuskeet, North Carolina

In the perfectly flat farmland between the Albemarle and the Pamlico, in North Carolina's Hyde County, there was once a long-lasting peat bog fire, according to Indian legend. A huge soup bowl was burnt out of the peat, and this was followed by a series of dry years. The dried peat disintegrated into dust and blew away with the changing winds. The bowl deepened, but not by much.

Then North Carolina reverted to character and the rains came. They are still coming. The big soup bowl became Lake Mattamuskeet, 40,000 acres of very shallow water, the two to three feet deep kind that waterfowl love. Waterfowl moved in, seemingly to stay. It became an important wintering spot for ducks, geese and tundra swans. They fed in the shallows and occasionally forayed out to feed on rich farm fields nearby.

But the land under the water was rich also, and that lured the state to try to drain it in 1909. North Carolina rains defeated that attempt.

Millionaire August Hecksher tried again in 1925, working with pumps capable of pumping a million gallons of water every four minutes! Hecksher thought he had succeeded. He started the town of New Holland and planted crops all over what had been Lake Mattamuskeet. He grew crops, but things kept going wrong, for Hecksher was fighting Mother Nature for the soul of Mattamuskeet. Rains kept his pumps busy all the time, and they proved unreliable.

Hecksher surrendered in 1933, just when the federal government had begun its search for suitable waterfowl areas—led by Ding Darling and Franklin Delano Roosevelt. The government bought it in 1934 and let it fill again. Mattamuskeet had won. Canada geese knew it, and they came to spend the winter. In 1935 there were 12,000, but that number grew exponentially. 1937 found 48,000 Canadas there and in 1958 105,000 Canadas lured hunters to the State-managed goose blinds operated on portions of the refuge. As many as 131,000 Canada geese wintered there from 1959 through 1968.

Then it ended with a calamitous crash in numbers in 1969. Public hunts ended in the 1972–1973 season. The hunting lodge (once a pumping station) was closed. What caused this end to the idyll?

Best guess is that the great flocks simply stopped farther north, on the Delmarva Peninsula. Why? Because Delmarva farming was turning

Greater snow geese and Canada geese winging over the marsh at Mattamuskeet, North Carolina.

North Carolina gunning for greater snow geese.

away from truck garden to corn and soybeans. At the same time, Carolina farmers were moving into earlier maturing corn crops—crops which were maturing and being harvested before the migrating geese arrived. Finding lots of food in Maryland, the geese simply stopped traveling the other 300 miles down to Mattamuskeet. Hunting pressure seemingly had nothing to do with it. The goose populations of the eastern seacoast were increasing by leaps and bounds during the time that Mattamuskeet lost its tens of thousands. The geese were alive, but they lived farther north. That's all.

Don't get me wrong—Mattamuskeet is still a good place to hunt geese. But its twenty year run as the star of all goosehunting places ended in 1968. It was great while it lasted. Perhaps the goose populations of Mattamuskeet might be rebuilt by captive flocks, rearing their young there? Who knows?

Once a pumping station, then a hunting lodge, this building at Mattamuskeet, North Carolina, is a reminder of the legendary hunting days.

Successful North Carolina hunters with mature and immature greater snow geese.

Remington Farms, Maryland

Back in 1944, Glen L. Martin, the airplane magnate, bought 3,000 acres of prime farmland near Chestertown, Maryland. He used it as a private hunting preserve—most of it. Some of it (only 16 acres) was kept in an inviolate sanctuary for the Canada geese which wintered thereabouts. No one shot on the sanctuary, and no one ever has right up to the present.

Martin's friends and acquaintances were invited to hunt on the farm when it suited Martin's fancy. Considering the size of the farm, the kill was never very heavy. The wintering flock grew and prospered.

In 1956, Remington Arms bought the farm and began farming it for maximum production of farm crops and wildlife. Food plantings of a permanent nature were begun, and crop rotations were planned which would ensure the permanence of the rich soils, while making the area more attractive to all forms of wildlife. The results were amazing and immediate. Over the years, this area has benefited greatly from the expert management provided by four managers—Dr. Joe Linduska,

Chuck Cadieux with Canadas taken on Remington Farms in Maryland.

Clark Webster, George Berger and Hugh Galbreath, who now operates the wildlife showcase. There is no way you can buy your way in to hunt there. You have to be invited.

In addition to providing excellent food and excellent habitat conditions for wintering geese, the continued success of the program at Remington Farms depends greatly upon the spare shooting schedule—which allows the birds much time to settle down again after each hunt. The total number of wintering birds continues to rise with the total wintering population of the Eastern Shore—now the biggest concentration of wintering Canada geese in the world, right near some twenty-five million people concentrated in cities like Baltimore and Washington.

I've been privileged to hunt at Remington Farms twice in my mis-spent life. What made each hunt so memorable was the treatment each hunter received from the staff. First of all, we were fed royally at the Farm the night before our hunt began. There was a cook named Peggy Thomson in those days, and she simply could not be beat. Oysters on the half shell and crab cakes were only preludes to Peggy's main entrée, and all the trimmings were perfect. Then we spent the evening lying to one another about other hunts in other coverts before going up to bed in the dormitories of the lodge. If you are able to go to sleep with a thundering mélange of snores assailing your ears, you slept blissfully. On my first visit I was lucky enough to draw a little side bedroom and was the only sleeper there. It sure was nicer to be lulled to sleep by the melodious honking of thousands of Canadas trading back and forth in the bright moonlight.

Before daybreak we were lured down to the breakfast table for bacon, ham and sausages, fried eggs, pancakes, muffins with melted butter and honey, hash browns and mugs of coffee—black and strong to start the day right. Each pair of hunters was assigned to a guide, and each guide put a black Labrador in the panel truck before he put the hunters in. Each of us carried a Remington Model 1100, and a box of steel shot (these were the days before steel was required anywhere, but Remington was ready). The blinds were built of corn stalks interlaced in a chicken wire front and elevated to allow the hunter to see over the tops of the standing corn. There was a plank seat and a shelf to hold the box of shells.

We had sporty shooting on mallards early on, but the geese didn't start our way until about nine. Then the sky filled with honkers for the next three quarters of an hour. As we picked our targets and dropped the geese, we saw the black Lab retrieving the birds with speed and skill under the direction of a guide named Don Travis. Don knew when we had filled out limits of ducks and geese, and he came to take us back to the lodge for mid-morning coffee.

I elected a nap before lunch, then made a glutton of myself again at Miss Peggy's table. In the early afternoon we hunted cottontails with beagles, bagging a few pairs of bunnies out of the multiflora rose jungle which the farm had provided to make life safer for the cottontails. We used Remington autoloaders again, but these were 20 gauge as befitted the smaller game. While we were cottontail hunting, others took their chances on the clay bird games—one known as "protection" and the other called many names, most of them unprintable. Both were excellent training for the game shooter.

The last two hours of the legal shooting time was spent in pit blinds, known as Smittys by those who still lacked the limit of geese. I tried pheasants and saw a dozen roosters, but failed to get a shot. Cover was a big protective factor for the wily ringnecks.

The next morning, we repeated our goose hunt, with similar results. Back at the lodge for mid-morning coffee, I found that the employees of Remington Farms had picked my birds and sharp-frozen them, tagging each package with my name and address and hunting license number. You cannot beat that kind of treatment. It is nice to learn how kings and emperors are treated, and it is nice to experience the great shooting opportunity offered by Remington Farms.

The real importance of Remington Farms lies in its work as a demonstration unit, a place where wise management has proved that a productive, "working" farm can be a wildlife paradise at the same time. Graduate students in wildlife management come here to study, and busloads of school children descend upon the farm almost every day of the year, to observe and learn from the example of Remington Farms.

As long as the overall population of wintering Canadas remains healthy, and as long as management continues to consider the needs of wintering geese, Remington Farms will undoubtedly continue to be the mecca for Canada goose hunters.

Forney Lake, Iowa

The area stretching from Forney Lake in southwestern Iowa to the other side of the Squaw Creek National Wildlife Refuge in northwestern Missouri was nominated by veteran goose hunter and wildlife writer Wilbur Horine, of Nevada, Iowa. His tales of Squaw Creek and Forney Lake brought back many memories to me, memories of the day when I was a beginning Federal Game Management Agent stationed in Sioux City, Iowa.

I don't know if Forney Lake was ever really a lake. In 1954 when I first got there, it was a fertile cornfield in the bowl-shaped flood plain of the Missouri River. There I worked with a giant of a man, Dutch Lemke, who was the local Iowa Conservation Officer. We had help from neighboring officers and other feds during the spring migration, when as many as 300,000 blues and snows (mostly snows in those days) used Forney Lake as a staging area after leaving Squaw Creek on their northward flight. I'm pleased to learn from Wilbur that the head count last fall in this area was 450,000 blues and snows—about half blues today.

There was lots of illegal spring shooting in this area 33 years ago, and the local gentry saw little reason to curtail their sport—after all, the geese were in great shape despite the poaching. I once took a pair of farm boys in to a local judge in Missouri. The miscreants pleaded guilty and the judge suspended their fine and jail sentence. Then he ordered me to return the geese they had illegally killed. His attitude was, "Don't bother me with such unimportant cases!"

This attitude quickly changed with the rise of local wildlife clubs, and with the coming of good law enforcement, both state and federal. This is the place where I followed an eighty-year-old man carrying a double-barrelled shotgun through a snowstorm as he walked toward a third of a million snow geese. He finally noticed me walking in plain sight behind him and stopped to see who I was and what I wanted. When I identified myself as a Game Agent, I asked him what he had in mind. "Well, sonny, "he said," I had thought to get a goose for Easter, but I don't think I will."

Strangely enough, hunting pressure was never heavy on this area thirty years ago, and Wilbur Horine reports that it is still not heavily hunted. The great majority of the wintering geese are blues and snows, with a smattering of Canadas and a few whitefronts thrown in. Most of the birds winter on Squaw Creek Refuge now, but they feed out over all of the surrounding country, in Missouri and in Iowa. Sporty pass shooting is enjoyed where the birds swing up and over the Loess hills on the east side of the Missouri River valley. Decoys and calls work well in the cornfields which cover most of this rich farm land.

Wilbur's advice on hunting this legendary goose area: Take Interstate 29 south from Council Bluffs, Iowa to Exit 20 onto Iowa #145 to Thurman, Iowa. Forney Lake is about two miles north. There are a number of blinds operated by the Iowa Conservation Commission. The river valley of the Nishnabotna River is also a favored feeding area and you might wish to check out these bottoms on the East Nishnabotna near Riverton, Iowa, about 15 miles south of Forney Lake.

Remember that you are hunting on or near the Iowa-Missouri state boundary and make sure that you hold the right license for the area you are hunting. Personnel of Squaw Creek National Wildlife Refuge five miles southeast of Mound City, Missouri, will assist you with the latest information as to where the geese are "using".

Good luck is had by following the geese from the refuge to feeding areas; then asking for permission to hunt on those feeding areas the next morning. Here are some names to contact for permission to hunt in commercial pits and blinds—

Joe Laukemper Laukemper Motor Company, Mound City, MO 64470.

John Dougherty Mound City, MO 64470.

Robert Rother Schoonover Oil Company, Mound City, MO 64470.

Buster Johns Mound City, MO 64470.

You can get an attractive brochure about the area by writing the Squaw Creek National Wildlife Refuge, Mound City, MO 64470.

James Bay, Canada

A very large part of the eastern Canada goose population—Canadas and lesser snows together—concentrate on the eastern shores of James Bay in the fall, gathering into huge flocks which make the flight south to wintering grounds. Some of the Canadas, and all of the "young of the year" snows and blues, have never seen a human being until they come

49

to James Bay in mid-September. As a result, they don't know about shotguns and shotgunners. With big concentrations of geese and näive youngsters all over the place, it is relatively simple to bag a limit. In years past, Cree Indians earned a reputation as expert callers—using only their own vocal cords and a cupped hand to form the melodious notes which fooled the James Bay geese so completely. Later on we realized that these callers didn't really have to be very good, they just had a bunch of youngsters (suckers for the call) to work on.

The hunting takes place on tundra, with very little chance to build a blind, and very little reason for having a blind. The Indian guides cut wings off the first few snow geese shot and fan the wing feathers out over a clod of mud, and those are your decoys. Sometimes the expert guides will prop up the head of a dead goose to make a more lifelike appearing deek. But shooting is fast and furious, for the birds are many and the caution has not yet been learned. James Bay has always been a fantastic place to hunt geese. Now with goose populations nearing modern time records, the hunting simply has to be even better.

Southern Saskatchewan

Wilf Pyle, knowledgeable outdoor writer with the Regina, Saskatchewan, *Leader-Post Daily*, nominates the area south of Kindersley and Rosetown, down to the South Saskatchewan River and the wide grain fields on both sides of that river. Historically this has been perhaps the best goose hunting in Canada, where good hunting is commonplace.

Hunting methods here include digging pits on the perimeter of feeding areas. Saskatchewan farmers are still a lot more friendly to hunters than we U.S.A. shooters are accustomed to. Often you can walk in to a good goose area and get permission to hunt from the landowner, without paying for the privilege.

I remember this area well from the days when I banded ducks and geese in Saskatchewan as an employee of the U.S. Fish and Wildlife Service. The geese will be there at the beginning of the season and the shooting will continue until weather calls a halt to it. Wilf Pyle points out that Saskatchewan has "Rural Municipalities" rather than counties, and that the good hunting is in RM's #166, 167, 226, 228, 259, 260

Snow geese take off from a loafing area along the south Saskatchewan.

Feathers from snow geese tip the hunter to a snow goose feeding area.

Gary Cortus and Ted Weins hold a limit of whitefronted geese from southern Saskatchewan.

Ted Weins with a whitefronted goose from southern Saskatchewan.

and (in some years) 261. These rural municipality numbers are clearly marked on the official Saskatchewan highway map, which does make it easy to find your way into some of the best goose hunting in the world. You don't really need a guide; but if you want one, Wilf Pyle has furnished a few names and addresses of the best guides in the business. These are found in Chapter 19. By the way, in addition to the geese, Saskatchewan offers sharptailed grouse, ducks and hungarian partridge to the shotgunner.

Two Buttes, Colorado

Back in the 1950's and early 1960's it was common to have as many as 60,000 Canada geese wintering in Prowers County, in the southeastern part of Colorado. Lamar was the center of goose hunting, the hub of activity around water areas such as Eads Lake to the north, John Martin Reservoir to the east and Two Buttes Reservoir and Turks's Pond to the south.

The biggest attraction was Two Buttes Reservoir, which had a lot of water in it in those good old days. Nearby Turk's Pond was a sanctuary, as the owner did not allow hunting on it. As a result, geese did a lot of trading back and forth from Two Buttes to Turk's Pond, and there was good shooting along the firing lines near each reservoir. This was corn country in those days, and the yellow corn was, as it is today, a prime attraction to the wintering Canadas.

Jack Grieb, respected waterfowl biologist who later led the Colorado Department, says that there were three sub-species of Canada in that wintering flock. Ninety percent of the geese were the lesser Canada, averaging about six pounds in weight. The other ten percent was the large honker, averaging about ten pounds, and the little Hutchens goose, which averages about three and a half pounds. Most of these birds were hatched in the MacKenzie River country on the Arctic Circle east of Alaska, in Canada.

Canadian hunters got first crack at these Canadas, which seems logical. About half of the annual kill was accomplished in the Kindersley Lake country, about halfway down the migration path. Coloradoans bagged approximately 28% of the annual kill, and much of this kill was centered on the Two Buttes Reservoir area. A very small portion of this flock went on into the northeastern corner of New Mexico and a few more went on down into Texas.

The Colorado State Department operated a public hunting area on Two Buttes and hunting was good. But the number of hunters increased every year, and the privilege of using the public hunting area was sadly abused. Finally, the state department began a system of regulating the area by charging a nominal fee (sounds silly today, but it was fifty cents when they began charging), and making all hunters check in and out, making them hunt only from their blinds, and respect all the hunting regulations.

But Two Buttes hunting went downhill. The flock was never overharvested, but the agricultural practices changed—shifting from corn to wheat. Corn was preferred by the geese. At about this time, the portion of the flock which went on down into New Mexico actually grew temporarily—at least, a larger percentage of this population went into New Mexico and hunting was better around places like Wagon Mound. However, New Mexico did not have any large reservoirs to offer; so there was no real lure to hold the birds in the Land of Enchantment.

Another bigger change was taking place in Colorado. The establishment of a large wintering population in north-central Colorado was succeeding, and wintering populations of this flock grew to as many as 80,000 Canada geese. This flock comes from southern Alberta and southern Saskatchewan with a contribution from northeastern Montana. Most of these winter in the Denver to Fort Collins to Greeley area, but about 20 percent of them are moving farther southeastward to Two Buttes.

As the so-called HiLine flock grows (and it has been growing steadily), it may exceed the wintering capacity of the north central Colorado area and again pump birds on down into the Two Buttes area. We may see the return of the good old days. True, there are more geese in the northeast than in the southeast portion of Colorado, but there is limited public access to the birds in the northeast.

Although we have experienced far greater than normal snow melt runoff in this portion of Colorado, Two Buttes Reservoir has been often starved for water. Irrigation dikes and water retention structures now steal most of the water before it ever gets to Two Buttes. The best thing that could happen to Two Buttes would be a series of flash floods, which might fill it again. In any event, Two Buttes is one of the good old places to hunt geese, and chances are good that it might regain its place as Colorado's best goose hunting spot—given enough water and the continued buildup of Canadas.

The Two Dakotas

As a tyro in the world of goose hunting, growing up in North Dakota, the top spot in the state was in the Devils Lake, Lake Alice-Lac Aux Morts region in northeastern Dakotaland. The hunting was mostly Canadas, for the growing hordes of lesser snow geese often overflew North Dakota entirely. Long flights by those white birds are nothing new. When weather conditions light a fuse under their tail feathers, they've been known to make it from James Bay all the way to the Texas Gulf Coast in four days of flying. By any reckoning, that is moving on. But the Dakotas were famed for sharptails, for prairie chicken, and for myriads of ducks, and really not that well-known as goose spots. Devils Lake was a big lake when I was a kid. It had once carried a steamboat

Most goose hunting in the Dakotas is accomplished in stubblefields.

upon its wide but shallow expanse. It provided the essential large water areas which geese need to keep them around. There was very little corn that far north; the area was famed for producing some of the finest durum wheat in the nation. But we found excellent goose hunting, especially for Canadas, on the shore lines of the sprawling lake. We got into the geese, still not veterans of hunting dangers, as they flew out to feed. Sometimes we really got into them.

Then came the dustbowl years and the Dakotas were hard hit. The waters of Devils Lake shrank to the point where all fish life died in the then small lake. Waterfowl numbers shrank at the same time—during the desperate years of 1931–1941. How about now? Is the Devils Lake area a hot spot of goose hunting?

Not really. Water areas are now plentiful across both Dakotas due to the dam-building propensities of the Corps of Engineers and the Bureau of Reclamation. Three decades of good precipitation have replenished the water levels across both states, and Devils Lake has grown to become a mighty lake again. But it now has competition from two hundred other large water areas, and the hunting opportunities have spread out. Now Devils Lake is just one of many good places in which to hunt geese. And, luckily, the geese have increased to match the increase in water areas.

Are the Dakotas good places to hunt geese? They sure are. But Devils Lake is not **the** hot spot of yore. No one puts it better than Chuck Post, Information Chief for the South Dakota department. I asked him if he could nominate any place in the lower Dakotas as one of the legendary spots. He said, "For geese? No way. For goose hunters the good old days are now." Most hunting in the Dakotas is stubblefield or cornfield hunting, usually from pit blinds or from "layouts" where the hunter covers himself with camouflage and lies alongside his decoys. While the geese are in, this hunting is hard to beat.

The Pas, Manitoba

Jimmy Robinson, the dean of all waterfowlers in the United States, nominates hunting on the Saskatchewan River, near The Pas as the best he's ever had. He has been the waterfowl hunting and shotgunning editor of Sports Afield for 60 years, which gives him a real vantage point from which to select the top spot. Jimmy, now 89 years old, has hunted geese in Western Canada, Mexico, Louisiana, Maryland, Ohio, Illinois, the Dakotas, California, Wisconsin, Minnesota, Hudson's Bay and a lot of way stations in between.

Jimmy says that his greatest hunt was near The Pas in 1938 when eight hunters in his party got 105 geese in three days—all Canadas. He has hunted these fields, shooting geese over decoys for more than forty years, and proclaims that it still rates the "legendary" description. The lure of this spot is still great, for 89-year-old Jimmy still goes there every fall for the opener in Manitoba. Jimmy has a lodge on Lake Manitoba which usually can offer 300,000 blues and snows on display during the fall migration. He has operated this lodge with his wife Clara since 1935. It is one of the legends of goose and duck hunting.

Where I Grew Up

Will you excuse me if I report on a legendary waterfowling spot? After all, I've been talking about the other guys quite a bit in this chapter. My home town was Jamestown, North Dakota. Jamestown lies on the James River, approximately 100 miles west of Fargo and 100 miles east of Bismarck. It is an important stop on the railroad, which was called the Northern Pacific when my father and grandfather and I worked for it. Now it's part of the Burlington Northern.

I'd like to think that Jamestown was the center of a legendary waterfowling area which stretched from central and western Saskatchewan and a bit of eastern Alberta, down across both Dakotas, a piece each of Minnesota and Montana; most of Nebraska and the northwestern corner of Iowa. Across that huge area prairie potholes provided homes to millions of nesting waterfowl—ducks as well as geese, before the plow came along and broke the plains. How good was the hunting? I'm glad you asked.

In 1923 a man named William B. Mershon published a book, *Recollections of My Fifty Years Hunting and Fishing*, through the Stratford Company of Boston, Massachusetts. Now this man Mershon was a goose hunter, and he evidently had a few bucks besides. In 1883, he reports that he bought a railroad car from a bankrupt circus. He had it rebuilt as a hunting lodge, dubbed it the "City of Saginaw" and went hunting with the lucky companions he invited along. At first he went deer hunting with it, and stayed in Michigan. Then he made the mistake of taking a private car trip to Yellowstone park. On the way he saw the waterfowl of North Dakota. Now, this man could afford to hunt anywhere he wanted to hunt. Where did he hunt? He made many trips to Buffalo, North Dakota, about fifty miles east of my home town. He also made many trips to Dawson, about fifty miles west of my home town. I commend him for his judgement.

Here's a quote from Mershon's book, "The railroads were lenient and generous in those days, and it was far cheaper for us to travel in this way, taking along our own cook and porter and provisions, than it would have been to have gone without the car."

In 1894, they built a new car, more luxurious than the earlier versions. They formed the Field and Stream Limited, with ten members. This rig could carry 500 gallons of fresh water and 750 pounds of ice—for this was before refrigeration.

Hunting geese at Dawson, N.D. Mershon wrote, "The plan was to drive through the stubble fields early in the morning and find where the geese were feeding, make an examination of the ground after the geese had left and see if there was much food left, or if they had been feeding there long, which could be told by the droppings or feathers and—if we had good reason to believe it was a regular feeding, we put in pits. Metal profile decoys were used and it was no uncommon thing to kill fifty or sixty geese in one afternoon's or morning's shoot. . .

"The biggest shoot we ever had was sometime in the early 80's on the Troy farm near Tappan, the station just east of Dawson on the Northern Pacific. It was a stormy day; snow squalls all day long. The geese were flying all day, thousands upon thousands of them. We killed 163 that day (five hunters: author). . .

"That night we drove eight miles back to Dawson and it was cold and we were wet. We all stuck our legs down in the geese and the warmth of their bodies kept us comfortable. We frequently brought home three hundred or more geese with us, and the arrival of the car in Saginaw was known in advance and our friends by the score flocked to the car to share in our bag. Not a bird was ever wasted, and these wheat field fed young geese were very highly considered for the table." End of quotation from Mershon.

In another part of this fascinating book, Mershon tells of hunting at Alkali Lake, which I well remember hunting with my father in about 1926. He wrote, "Ducks and geese covered the surface. I have never seen such clouds of water fowl. When taking wing the roar was like thunder; they would circle around and settle in another part of the lake." Hunting at Alkali Lake was never that good from 1926 through 1954, the years when I hunted North Dakota intensively, but the great variety of waterfowl reported by Mershon still held true. He tells of shooting "one yellow-legged fellow that the natives called a California goose, with a breast all blotched with black." This was undoubtedly a whitefront, or specklebelly. They still migrate through North Dakota, but their numbers are greatly reduced. The bag that contained the whitefront added up to 58 geese, which was a fair afternoon's shoot for five guns. It seems that Mershon adhered to the slogan, "if it dies—it fries." He tells about drawing the geese and expressing them to friends in St. Paul on the railroad.

Yes, there were lots of waterfowl on the Dakota prairies in the late 1800's. Consider Mershons words again, "I remember standing on the edge of the Sam Devore Slough when something alarmed the waterfowl and they fairly darkened the sky when they got up, and the roar re-minded one of a heavy train moving at a rapid rate of speed over a long, resonant trestle." And it was not only the geese, Dakota duck shooting was also great—conceivably better than the goose shooting. In one hour and a half, Mershon sat on a soap box to keep his butt dry and shot 46 ducks and one snow goose. He ends his narrative sadly with the words, "There were no laws regarding shipment of game out of the state and we were able to bring home a fine lot of birds to our friends. We commenced going to Dawson with the car Saginaw, a year after we discovered it in 1884 and we went every year until 1899."

Mershon claims that the goose hunting around Dawson petered out in 1900 and they moved north to Devils Lake, North Dakota; and finally went on up to near Moose Jaw, Saskatchewan.

Obviously I was not to the manor born. I got only Mershon's leav-ings by coming along fifty years too late. I didn't hunt from a private car but walked out of Jamestown on two feet, or (later on) rode out in a Model T, and even later, in a Model A. But I had a better gun and better shells than he did, so there. The waterfowl hunting I found while growing up in the Dakotas, from 1926 when I first accompanied my dad, until 1954 when I left the home state, was wonderful.

Out near Dawson, where Mershon hunted, we found Canada geese roosting on what we called the "Railroad Slough", because a Northern Pacific embankment ran right through the middle of it. My brothers and I would hide along the embankment and pass shoot. We got excellent luck when a passing train roiled the geese—they circled and we shot. Mershon, you and I shared a legendary goose hunting spot.

Skagit Flats, Washington

Veteran outdoorsman-cinematographer Howard Gray nominated the Skagit Flats on Washington's Pacific Coast, as one of the legendary hunting spots. The attraction here is a big flock of lesser snow geese, hatched on Wrangel Island in Russia's Siberia. Who said nothing good ever came out of Communist Russia? In times past, this flock has numbered about 25,000 wintering birds each year. In 1985–1986 wintering season this number mushroomed up to the 40,000 mark. This made for excellent hunting, and increased the annual kill from an average of about 3,000 to nearer 5,000. If there's a good nesting season on Wrangel, there's good hunting on the Skagit Flats. It has always been this way, and—the good Lord willing—it will always be this way. The State Department of Game owns about 10,000 acres of the Delta—and all of this land is open to the public. Skagit Flats is a very popular place to hunt and each year records the highest wintering populations and the highest goose harvest in western Washington.

Southern Illinois

My friend Jack Ehresman, outdoor writer for the Peoria *Journal Star*, nominates one of the most famous of all spots. Jack gets so eloquent in talking about it, let's print his letter in full:

"Southern Illinois, particularly the Cairo area and Horseshoe Lake, has been one of the legendary Canada goose hunting meccas in the country for more than a century.

Waterfowlers from many states have made the journey to these bottomlands along the Mississippi River, enjoyed the warm hospitality and more often than not gone home with a honker or two. Canada geese and the men who chased them have become as much a part of the colorful history of the area as the river boats and its Shawnee Hills.

Hunting wild geese on sand bars of the Mississippi was documented as early as 1855 in Colonel Peter Hawke's book, *Guns and Shooting*. And there are stories of General U.S. Grant and some of his troops, while quartering in Cairo, supplemented their rather bland military rations with Canada honkers from the nearby river.

Private clubs began forming during the early years of the 20th century. Records indicate the earliest operation, known as the Egyptian Hunting and Fishing Club, began in 1904. Membership totalled 50; dues were five bucks.

By 1915, 15 clubs were operating along the river near McClure, Ware, Reynoldsville, and Wolf Lake. It is said that many of the club-houses were burned by bootleggers—for this was prime country for both geese and illegal stills during Prohibition Days.

In 1927, the Illinois Department of Conservation purchased 3,500 acres around Horseshoe Lake, an old ox-bow of the Mississippi near Olive Branch, 15 miles northwest of Cairo where the Ohio joins the Mississippi. The purchase of Horseshoe and its development turned out to be the most important happening in the history of Illinois' honker flock. That same year, dredging of sand bars began to channelize the Mississippi for navigation. Looking for a place to rest, the honkers all discovered Horseshoe. Soon commercial hunting clubs sprang up around Horseshoe, boosting an otherwise poor economy. Twenty-five of them still operate today.

In 1946, the entire Mississippi Flyway honker flock was reduced to just 55,000 birds, 22,000 of them wintering in Illinois. The entire flyway was closed to goose hunting. Additional sanctuaries were created . . . Crab Orchard NWR near Carbondale in 1947 and Union County NWR near Ware in 1950. These added areas dispersed the flocks and spread out the hunting.

In 1950, when I began making my annual pilgrimages to the area, Horseshoe was the place to go and Cairo was the place to stay. Pits on the public hunting areas produced well. I can remember one morning when four of us bagged our eight geese in less than 30 minutes. I was so impressed that I took my young bride the next year. The temperature dropped to fifteen degrees and the geese never flew. My bride hasn't been goose hunting since.

Names of clubs back then included Worthington, Miller-Grace, Blakemore, Willis, Patton, Greenley, Farris, Marlin, Pecord and Yates. Many of these hospitable folk were colorful, and able to entertain with hunting yarns. With nicknames of "Spice", "Too Tall", and "Babe" nobody who ever met the Yates brothers would forget them. A fellow could hunt for ten bucks a day then.

Of course, everyone had to start the morning with a hunter breakfast at places like the Goose Pit or Les Grah's. And there was "Frog City"—an area between Cairo and Horseshoe. Its bright lights, games of chance and dancing girls made more than one hunter hurry to reach the pits by opening hour and that hunter often shot with a headache, besides.

As this book of Charlie's goes to press, the Canada goose flock has never looked healthier in Illinois, numbering upwards of half a million birds. Growing numbers of home-grown giant Canadas have increased to the point where local seasons have been held at various spots around the state, adding to a healthy flock which nests in the James and Hudson's Bay areas in northern Ontario.

Although hunters don't flock to Cairo as they once did and there is plenty of competition now for the "Goose Hunting Capitol of the World" title, Horseshoe Lake and this colorful area along the Mississippi is still the granddaddy of all goose hunting in the midwest. Maybe even in the nation. That history no one can erase."

Chapter 3

Goose Management

Sixty years ago, the wintering flock of Canada geese on the Eastern Shore of Chesapeake Bay was not as great as it is today. In most parts of this goose paradise, hunting was allowed every day of the open season. When the flocks find that they cannot let down into any fields without being shot at, when they find a shotgun hidden in every cornfield, those flocks move on to other—hopefully safer—pastures. As a result of this "unenlightened" system of hunting geese, the kill was very small, compared to what it is today. In addition, the heavy gunning along the Chester, the Oxford, Tred Avon, Tilghman Island, Crisfield, Deale, and Salisbury areas, served to harry the geese out of the area and they continued to migrate southward, some of them going all the way to northern Florida. Many of them furnished the wonderful gunning that is part of the history of Mattamuskett, North Carolina.

Then the moral of the story began to soak in. If you didn't shoot *all* of the golden flock, it continued to provide hunting for all—in moderation.

Moderation! That was the word that explained it all. Gunning practices slowly changed on the landed manors of the Eastern Shore. If you shot over your fields only on Monday morning and Thursday afternoon, and left the birds alone the remainder of the week, you had good shooting every time you ventured forth from the first day through the last day of the season.

Some variation of this shooting schedule is now observed almost everywhere in the bigger holdings along the Eastern Shore. Obviously it works. The wintering flocks no longer go on down the Atlantic Seaboard.

Missourians are from the "show me" state, and they don't take kindly to accusations without proof. When they are accused of shortstopping the geese which formerly went on south to winter in Louisiana, they come up with a denial and a counter charge.

Advocates of the shortstopping theory hold that Missouri has made its wintering grounds so attractive to the big birds that they don't go farther south. Missourians counter with a different explanation. The gospel according to Missouri is this: In olden days a few geese wintered in Missouri and many geese wintered in Louisiana and Texas. Over the decades, Missouri harvested a small percentage of their wintering birds, so their flocks increased and prospered. At the same time (according to the Missouri theory) Louisiana and Texas shot so many of their flock each winter that fewer and fewer birds *existed* to make the long flight to the Gulf Coast each year. Hence, their wintering flocks decreased. Stating this hypothesis will get you a roar of argument anywhere south of the Mason-Dixon line, but I feel that the Missourians are at least partly correct. The first time I ever heard this argument broached, its proponent was a Canadian biologist who had no stake in the debate. In fact, he had a wonderful opportunity to observe the argument from afar. He also refused to espouse his own theory in public, stating that he did not want to start another war between North and South.

Sometimes "shortstopping" is the result of efforts to establish resident flocks. Colorado has done a magnificent job of establishing breeding flocks of resident Canadas along the front range of the Rocky

Mountains for about 100 miles, starting in the southern suburbs of Denver and reaching north.

Using captured wild birds, they released wing-clipped pairs on suitable nesting habitat and provided good nesting spots that the birds could reach. The results have been astonishing. It is pleasant now, when I visit my daughter in Denver, to awaken to the mellifluous honking of large flocks of Canadas as they fly out from Kendricks Lake roosting areas to feed in the back yards of the suburbanites. Geese stroll across the fairways of many of Denver-area golf courses, and crop the lawns in Edgewood, Littleton and other Denver suburbs. These geese stay inside the city, which functions as a refuge. They are seldom shot at. But the presence of these flocks of fat and happy home-grown honkers serve as very efficient live decoys to attract migrating birds. The winter population here greatly exceeds the summer population which explains the decrease in wintering Canadas in New Mexico. Colorado's intent had nothing to do with shortstopping, but New Mexico's geese have been shortstopped, nevertheless. Remember, if New Mexico improves conditions for Canadas in the Land of Enchantment, it will have no effect upon those shortstopped flocks, for they will never come down to New Mexico to see what is available to them.

But greatly improved conditions on National Wildlife Refuges, such as Horicon Marsh, Horseshoe, Necedah, Union Slough, Squaw Creek, Brigantine, Blackwater and countless others has done much to shortstop the geese. These attractive refuges pile up the wintering populations and set up hunting conditions which can best be described as slaughter pens. In some areas, a goose blind just outside the refuge fence is a lethal method of harvesting geese. If you can get your gun into one of those blinds, you automatically have a limit of Canadas. This degrades the sport but has little to do with the management of geese. In order to limit the kill, quotas are set up, and the federal government closes the season in that area when their surveys show that a certain number of geese has been killed in that area. This is fine and dandy for the geese, and it provides a financial windfall for the owners of land abutting the refuge. It also arouses the ire of the sportsman who has set his vacation for the latter half of the goose season, intending to hunt geese—and finds the season closed (when the quota has been killed) before he starts his hunt.

Attempts to flush geese out of these northern refuges and send them along southward have failed almost 100%. Once the geese have become accustomed to eating the yellow corn of the refuge fields and surrounding farm fields, they simply will not leave. Harrying with aircraft has proved futile and dangerous to the pilots of the aircraft. Carbide exploders are effective in keeping a flock out of a certain field, but will not run them out once they've become established there. Scarecrows are (statistically) worthless, although they might seem to have a small, localized effect.

Dense concentrations of wintering geese worry waterfowl biologists, for these concentrations are "just asking for it" as far as waterfowl diseases are concerned. Perhaps after we suffer the loss of an entire flock we will start serious work on solving this problem. Today we do have a problem.

Man's management of goose migrations has been tremendously effective where the Canada goose is concerned. This does not mean that the big Canadas are the dumb and easily domesticated members of their family. Far from it! It does mean that they are smart enough to recognize a good thing when they see it and take advantage of it.

Management must be aware of the big problem being posed by huge concentrations of geese. Concentration of mortality in one area to the detriment of others does no favor to anyone, least of all to the average goose hunter. We would be far better served by 100 flocks of 100 honkers each, providing some sport hunting to goosehunters in 100 different locations, than by the flock of ten thousand birds concentrated in one place. This concentration leads to degrading the hunting experience, unwanted over-regulation of the hunting privilege, dangers from disease, excessive claims of crop depredation and many other ills.

These are worries when you have a flock of ten thousand birds. Imagine what happens when the flock reaches 100,000 birds as it often does on the federal refuges in the Mississippi Flyway.

Moderation is the word here! Don't exceed the carrying capacity of your land area by piling too many geese upon it.

Moderation is also the word in planning the hunting of your own flock on your own land. Don't burn out the flock by shooting it every morning and evening. Geese are too smart for that; they'll leave quickly. Shoot only two (or at most three) days per week. That flock will stay as long as there's food available.

Chapter 4

Which Gun for Geese?

A goose is a trophy waterfowl for most of us. That trophy waterfowl deserves a clean, instantaneous death—as do all forms of wildlife which we hunt. Respect for the bird limits our choice of shotguns and gauges and charges of shot and powder that will give us the instantaneous kill. The same respect for the wild life limits our shots to those we can make 90% of the time, and leads the real sportsman to forego the "maybe" shot at a bird which is out of range.

You need a certain gun for pass shooting Canadas coming down wind at extreme altitude. You need an entirely different gun if shooting Canadas over decoys on the Eastern Shore, where the shot should be at 25 yards or even less.

But if you pin me down, I'd have to say that the best armament for goose hunting is a Remington 1100 Autoloader in three inch magnum, twelve gauge, full choke. In the hands of the average shot, that gun

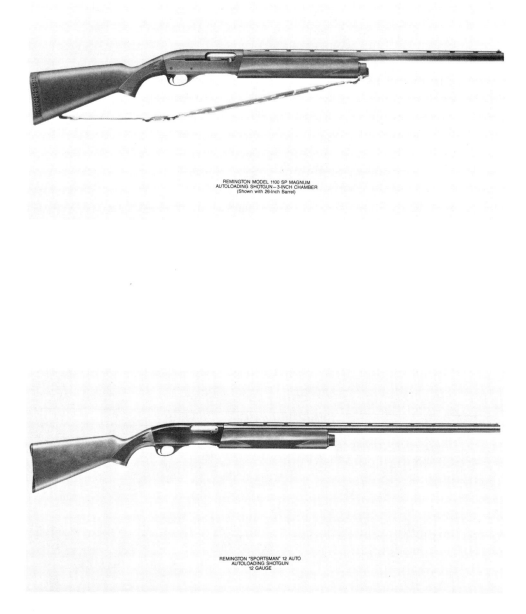

REMINGTON MODEL 1100 SP MAGNUM
AUTOLOADING SHOTGUN—3-INCH CHAMBER
(Shown with 26-Inch Barrel)

REMINGTON "SPORTSMAN" 12 AUTO
AUTOLOADING SHOTGUN
12 GAUGE

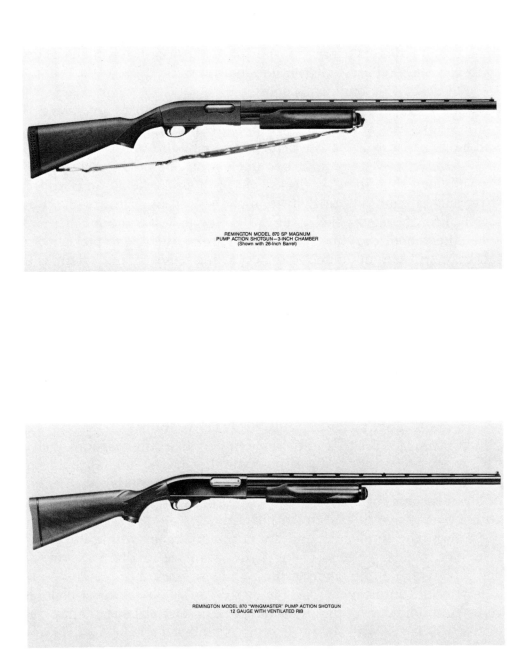

REMINGTON MODEL 870 SP MAGNUM
PUMP ACTION SHOTGUN—3-INCH CHAMBER
(Shown with 26-Inch Barrel)

REMINGTON MODEL 870 "WINGMASTER" PUMP ACTION SHOTGUN
12 GAUGE WITH VENTILATED RIB

71

should give clean kills 90% of the time at ranges up to 45 yards, with the percentage going down fast at longer ranges.

With that gun, in that gauge, I'd use #4 shot over decoys, in field or water situations. I'd use #2 shot on pass shooting—which occurs must less often on geese than it does on ducks.

But that's only one man's opinion.

One of my goose hunting friends who specializes in "bragging range" shots, uses a ten gauge with a 32 inch barrel. It's a single shot, and he makes sure of his aim before he touches off that roman candle of a shell. He is very good at extreme range, but he is sorely handicapped when shooting over deeks. That full choke "long tom" gun is firing such a tight pattern that he might as well use a thirty-oh-six at close range. He gets his jollies out of letting us lesser mortals fire our shots, then about the time that we are sending the dog to pick up the fallen, he will zero in on one of the departing geese—one that thinks it is already safely out of range, and brings it down with a single bellow of the blunderbuss. He uses #2 shot, *CopperKote*, in that cannon. He has seldom fired more than five shots in the same day—and that is good, because he might dislocate his shoulder if he fired more than that.

A ten gauge is a mighty weapon, and it executes geese with ease. You still have to hold it right and fire it right, and I feel that it has but a tiny advantage over the three inch magnum twelve gauge.

In third place is the 12 gauge firing 2¾ inch magnum shells.

In fourth place is the 12 gauge firing conventional shells.

In fifth place is the twenty gauge full choke firing magnum shells. This peashooter is not really a goose gun, but it has long range killing power—if you hit with it. It seldom wounds geese, for it is either a case of down it comes or missed it entirely. You might get the same results with a twenty-two rifle, also. I'm not sure.

I chose the autoloader, and I've been very happy with a Browning Five Shot for many years. There is no advantage in the five shot, of course, as you are only allowed three shots in the gun nowadays.

After the autoloaders, the side by side double is the most popular goose gun, followed by the over-under and in last place the pump. Of course, this is just with the goose hunters I know—I make no claim for statistical proof of that ranking.

Having grown up on shotguns with one sighting plane, I find it difficult to hit with a side by side. However, I realize that I am in the minority here. If I can ever afford another shotgun, it will be a Browning Citori Superposed (Over and under). I've shot that beauty a few times and have a severe case of the yearning for it.

Among the autoloaders, I feel that the Remington 1100 has the best reliability rating of all. At Mexico's hot spot, Rancho La Estancia, they furnish guns to their dudes, because of the red tape involved in getting your favorite blunderbuss into Mexico. They are a long ways from a gunsmith, so they must have reliability. They chose Remington 1100's exclusively. Why do I shoot a Browning, then? I got a very good deal on it about 25 years ago and fell in love with it. It has never malfunctioned in any way (despite some mighty rough treatment) over the quarter of a century that I've been carrying it.

In 1985, Remington tried to improve on the Model 1100. They introduced it in the 1100 SP Magnum version for waterfowlers (and turkey hunters). The metal is completely parkerized, giving it a non-reflective finish which does not gleam in the sunlight. They gave it a dull stock finish and even provided a camouflage carrying sling. At the same time they also brought out the old reliable Model 870 in the same dull finish and carrying three inch chambers for use with the bigger shells.

If you are a "one shotgun" man, and still want to be well-armed for geese, you might do well to consider a twelve gauge Model 870 with three inch chambers and the "REM" choke system. In that arrangement, you can shoot everything, using one ounce loads up to the three inch, $1\frac{7}{8}$ inch magnums. By changing the choke inserts, the owner of that combo can hunt upland game with improved cylinder, medium range with a modified choke and still have a full choke for long distance waterfowl.

Incidentally, because we will all be shooting steel shot exclusively in a few years, it is well to remember that Remington has a lot of experience and has done a lot of testing of the steel shot loads in their guns. Because they feel that muzzle velocity is of utmost importance in steel shot loads (you can't have satisfactory retained energy without high muzzle velocity), Remington has stuck with the one and a quarter steel shot load in their three inch steel loads. That combo provides the best killing power at longer ranges. They recommend number one steel shot for pass shooting, and number two steel shot for goose hunting over decoys.

Chapter 5

The Steel Shot Controversy

If there ever was a controversy which should have been buried long ago, it is the arguments about using lead shot in waterfowl areas. Two facts are admitted by everyone in this argument:

1. Lead shot kills birds by being ingested and ground up in their gizzards.

2. We have too few waterfowl, and we cannot afford to lose them when we do not have to.

In the words of Dorothy Parker's poem, "with that the gist and sum of it, what good will ever come of it?"

Let's go back and look at the history of this situation. About 1949, Frank Bellrose of the Illinois Natural History Foundation began a many-year study of lead poisoning in waterfowl. Too many birds—mostly ducks—were being found sick and dying of lead poisoning. The typical symptoms were emaciation which caused the breastbone to stick out

This lesser snow goose is a victim of lead poisoning. Not yet dead, it is too weak to even try to escape from the photographer.

razor sharp through the shrunken breast muscles, a nasty looking green discharge from the anus, and a listlessness which grew slowly worse as the bird starved to death. What was happening was that the lead was being ground up into fine particles by the churning action of the gizzard. The birds picked up the pellets, thinking they were seeds which were good to eat. The lead entered the blood stream and the birds' fate was sealed.

Waterfowlers who found birds in this condition often took them home and tried to feed them back to health. Most of the time it didn't work. Sometimes, if it was caught soon enough and if the birds were given lots of water and lots of green roughage to eat, they occasionally made it back to health.

As a game warden in North Dakota, and later as a Game Management Agent in Sioux City, Iowa, I brought in many lead-poisoned birds and wrapped them in plastic sacks and mailed them to Frank Bellrose. I had picked up these birds from the hiding places, back under the rushes, which they instinctively sought after becoming too sick to fly.

Bottom feeding ducks naturally suffered more from lead poisoning than did the grass-grazing, cornfield-feasting honkers or other geese.

Next set of facts: Lead shot sinks to the bottom in water and lies on top (temporarily) when fired over land. The more concentrated hunting, as in heavily hunted marshes, serves to concentrate the lead shot and make its ingestion more likely. Left alone, lead shot would sink out of sight in both marsh and field, in the normal processes of agriculture and the normal sedimentation in the sloughs. But the first year mortality was high.

We were losing many birds to lead poisoning. Granted by everyone. But there were enough birds to provide good sport, even with the steady mortality caused by lead poisoning. So nothing was done about it. But when populations got too low, the unit value of one waterfowl's life went way up. We could no longer afford the loss to lead poisoning, unless we wished to cut out the loss due to sport hunting. Given a choice, even the duck or goose would vote for a charge of #4's rather than the lingering horror of lead poisoning.

So the logical answer was to go to a shot pellet which did not contain lead. Okay, but that's not easy. Lead is a very heavy metal and its ballistic coefficients are good. In other words, because it is heavy it retains velocity for a good long distance from the muzzle of the gun. As you know, lead shot will kill a goose at sixty yards, if it is fired by an expert shotgunner who places the pellets where they belong. About 90% of all waterfowl, however, are shot at ranges of less than thirty yards.

The search for an acceptable substitute went on for many years, and the steel shot seemed to offer the best hope for a good substitute for lead. It rusted away quickly in the dampness of the waterfowl hunting grounds. Even if ingested and ground up in the gizzard, it had no lethal affects.

But retained velocity of steel shot is much lower than retained velocity of lead shot. Which simply means that the effective killing range of steel shot is less than we are accustomed to enjoying with lead shot. In the hands of an expert shot—lead shot will kill a goose at sixty yards, with the occasional record showing one killed at seventy yards. In the hands of that same expert shot, using steel shot, the goose is safe at sixty yards, because it will be deemed out of range by the expert. At fifty yards, it is an extreme range shot, which the expert might make. At forty yards, steel shot kills as dead as lead shot, in my opinion.

I was first introduced to steel shot when I was a guest at Remington Farms, Chestertown, Maryland. We were all given Remington 1100's and a box of steel shot before we went out to the goose blinds in the cold dawn. The limit was three, as I remember it—all dark geese, of course, for this is the Eastern Shore. I dropped three geese with three shots. No shot was over thirty-five yards, and all three birds dropped stone dead.

Later in the day, we had the chance to shoot at a few mallards that were from 45 to 55 yards out. I missed some, hit some, about my usual average. Then I asked for the chance to shoot steel shot at clay targets thrown on the fine trap range at Remington Farms. Purposely waiting until the birds were too far out, I shot almost zero on the long range ones. The steel shot did not carry out, as we put it, well enough to knock chunks off those distant clay pigeons. My opinion then, as my opinion today, is that steel shot **SHOULD** be used in all shooting at live birds. We cannot afford to waste ducks and geese to lead poisoning.

Opponents claim that there is increased crippling when steel is shot, because the pellets lack the killing impact of lead. They have a point here. Obviously steel is inferior to lead at long range. Which simply means one thing—**AVOID LONG RANGE SHOTS**. You owe it to the resource to avoid long shots if there is no chance that you'll kill cleanly.

The U.S. Fish and Wildlife Service had conducted many tests on steel shot, and had readied a movie about the coming changeover from lead to steel. But just before this movie was released, G. Ray Arnett took over as Interior's top wildlife man. He immediately quashed the informational movie. Ray is a good goosehunter, and a very knowledgeable man about wildlife. But I have never understood his stand on the steel shot issue.

The National Wildlife Federation chief, Jay Hair, immediately hollered foul and tried to force Interior to release the movie. He didn't succeed in getting the official release of the movie. Still, he succeeded in viewing a pirated version of the movie and telling the hunting fraternity what was contained in that movie. I had the interesting job of mediating a debate between G. Ray Arnett and Jay Hair at the annual Conference of the Outdoor Writers Association. Both men are excellent debaters, both are skilled speakers, neither are the least bit awed by the nature of the opposition.

In his presentation, Arnett said that the research results were inconclusive (research is almost always inconclusive which is why most research reports end with the words, "Further study is indicated"); that the killing effect of steel shot was not fairly estimated in the tests; that crippling losses would exceed the present lead poisoning losses.

Jay Hair made the telling point, time after time, that this was the Fish and Wildlife Service's own research, and questioned Arnett's motives for quashing publication of honest research. In my mind, Hair won the debate hands down over a very worthy opponent. Most of the audience reported that their views had not changed. If they were in favor of steel shot before the debate, they still were in favor. If they had been against steel shot before the debate, they were still against steel shot after the debate. Arnett went over to the National Rifle Association after his term in Interior, and he remains a vocal opponent to steel shot.

It should be obvious to anyone that steel shot is coming to all our waterfowl areas. The feds are steadily increasing the number and size of steel shot zones, and the states are slowly coming around to that view of inevitability. My objection to steel shot is not a good reason— I object because the steel shot is difficult to handload and, so far at least, is too expensive. But we will all be shooting steel shot soon, and wildlife will be the better for that change.

Chapter 6

Placement of Decoys

Fifty-five years of goose hunting have led me to the inescapable conclusion that there are no hard and fast rules as to how to place a decoy spread.

The closest thing we can have to a rule for decoy placement is this: When the wind is blowing enough to ruffle a goose's feathers, that goose faces into the wind so that the wind will flatten his feathers against his body instead of trying to pluck the feathers off.

The best teacher is a wild goose flock. Take every opportunity to observe their patterns of movement, how they space themselves and how they move without interfering with each other's "space". Karl Lorenz's studies of agression among greylag geese showed very definitely that there is a pecking order among geese. Every goose in the flock knows which goose he is superior to and which ones he must give way to. This pecking order is learned when the gosling is still quite young—each gosling learns its place in the ranking of the family. Later as families join together to form flocks prior to migration, the young gosling tries his hand at bluffing and charging—and in so doing, he establishes his place in the larger pecking order.

All this is to establish the fact that geese do not crowd themselves, unless they must. Canada geese, more dignified, more sedate, give themselves more room than do the more gregarious, more quarrelsome, noisier Lesser Snow Geese. Piling in to a cornfield, snow geese often land right on top of each other, jostle and push to get themselves some space. Canadas are less apt to do this, preferring to space themselves in a courteous manner.

This does not mean that you should place snow goose decoys closer together than you would place Canada decoys. Your purpose is to attract the attention of the goose flock, not to imitate reality. If we are using life size decoys (as opposed to oversize deeks), I feel that a minimum of five feet between decoys is a minimum. If the spacing is eight feet—in every direction—between decoys your spread will be more noticeable and—perhaps—more lifelike. Oversize deeks need more elbow room of course.

Many good goose hunters make use of a strategy to bring the incoming flock closer to the gun. They do this by leaving an opening in the spread so that the decoying birds will land in that opening—or at least head for that opening, bringing them within range of the gun. Such an opening should be at least forty feet across—at least forty feet between the decoys on either side.

But more important, the opening into which you wish to entice the geese should be within 20 yards of the gun muzzle. If you are hunting in a strong and steady wind, it will be wise to place your decoys well upwind of the blind. In this way, the incoming geese will come within point blank range of your gun when they are making their final approach to land. Don't place the decoys too far upwind, as you must be sure that the geese will be within range.

If the breeze is light or non-existent, it will be wise to have decoys on two or more sides of the blind. You cannot guarantee the heading the geese will come in on, so you must be ready to take the shot in any direction. It is usually better to have the open space (your landing target for decoying geese) about ten to twenty yards distant from the blind, not right on the blind. There is nothing more embarrassing than having a lone goose come in and land right on top of your pit blind, making the lid heavy enough to slow the action of throwing back the lid and getting your shot. Also, do not place a goose on (or very near) the blind. Instead of making your blind appear safer to the goose, you are simply putting up another obstacle to get in your way when you want to shoot. If it is within shotgun length, it will block your vision in those rare cases when geese actually land among the decoys. No sportsman would shoot a goose on the ground, naturally, but there have been times when I didn't give them a chance to get very far off the ground. This is especially true if the bird has landed at or near extreme shotgun range from your blind.

There is no reason to arrange your goose decoys in a horseshoe form, nor in a diamond pattern. Canada geese normally live their lives in family groupings—not in single file, nor in regimental array. I like to place a feeding group of six or seven Canadas near each other, as if they were a family unit. Then if there is room, put a dozen yards between that family group and the next family group. My next couple of families may be side by side, almost as if they were one family.

Placing solid goose decoys on a Rio Grande sand bar.

83

With snow geese decoys, the arrangement seems to be completely haphazard, with geese scattered all over hell's half acre. Leave a space for landing birds to come into, so that their final approach will bring them within gun range. Outside of that, successful snow goose decoying depends more upon quantity than quality—for the sociable, talkative snow and blue goose likes to join the crowd.

Feeding decoys, or alert decoys, or resting decoys? I frankly don't think it makes much difference. So I get an assortment—in case it does make a difference. After watching thousands of wild geese, I know that they are all feeding when they first go out to eat. But in a very short ten minutes some birds are standing motionless on one leg, or even lying down completely. Others are stretching their necks constantly, as if on watch—we romanticize the situation by calling them sentries. After the flock has been on the feeding site for half an hour, individuals assume all possible positions, some are still eating, some are sentries, some are asleep with their head laid back on the body, others are preening, stretching wing feathers out for inspection. Unless the wind is strong, they are facing in every conceivable direction, not standing at attention with beaks pointing into the breeze.

If there is an elevation of any kind within range of your blind, it is wise to put a decoy atop it. For example, a muskrat house, or a fallen over shock of corn. I've noticed that immature snows and blues, especially, like to be the "king of the hill". That is their reason for being on top of the elevated place; my reason for placing one there is to increase the visibility of the spread.

Don't crowd your decoys; yet remember that your shot string must be able to kill effectively at the outer edge of your decoy spread.

Place decoys haphazardly; but remember that geese stay in family groupings.

Experiment with different arrangements until you find one that you have confidence in; still remember that no goose turns his butt to a cold wind.

And there is one element that makes a decoy spread more attractive—a good call, properly blown.

The location of the decoy spread is important—perhaps more important than the location of individual decoys within the spread. For example, it is almost always true that geese will not land close to standing corn, nor to a tree line, nor to buildings. They fear that the conceal-

84

ment offered might allow a predator to hide within the standing corn, or in the trees where they might rush upon the goose when it is on the ground.

This is not to say that geese will never move into standing corn. I have seen them do this. However, they landed a good distance away from the standing corn and slowly, warily, walked over to the standing corn.

On my favorite goose watching area, the Bosque del Apache National Wildlife Refuge in New Mexico, there are many places where feeding fields run right up to the line of thick brush or trees. There is a healthy population of coyotes on the refuge, also. The interaction between coyote and snow goose is interesting to watch. A coyote will come out of the brush line, trotting along nonchalantly, trying to pretend that he has no interest in the thousands of white geese. Snow geese are always noisy, but when the coyote appears their din reaches new decibel readings. They also move warily away from the coyote, walking slowly but keeping an eye on the danger.

On three different occasions I've seen the coyote make a charge at the thousands of geese, hoping to bag one before they gained altitude. I've never seen it work. However, this strategy sometimes works for the coyote, for it shows him a dead or sick goose on the ground, which he can then run down for dinner. With as many as 60,000 snow geese on the refuge, natural mortality provides many dead birds every day, and the coyote helps the hawks and crows to clean up the carcasses.

This observation of coyote-goose behavior gives me a reason to place my decoys well away from concealment—concealment which could hide the goose's enemies.

Chapter 7

Decoys

Solid Goose Decoys

The decoy is an important part of the lore of goosehunting, and the wooden decoys made by market hunters before the advent of protective game laws are among the most effective of all lures, second only to live decoys. Full-bodied solid wooden decoys, life size, are heavy. A deep commitment to the sport is required to spend the time—or money—to outfit the hunter with a set of wooden solids. Properly carved and properly painted, they are the most effective of all artificials. Properly weighted, they float naturally and look very lifelike riding the waves. Hollowed-out full bodies were an improvement because of the reduced weight.

Unless you are a collector with money, the solid wooden decoy is out of reach.

Styrofoam solids are a cheap imitation, but very effective.

I once hunted over a set of cork full-bodied deeks that did the job.

Modern materials like fiberglass and plastics have made solids economical and light to carry. They lack the authenticity of the old wooden carved jobs, but the difference hasn't been noticed by the geese, to the best of my knowledge.

Shells

Because most geese are hunted on land, rather than over water, the shell decoy is the best possible choice. I have several sets of shells, two dozen in Canada goose persuasion and another couple dozen in snows and blues paint jobs. A noticeable absence is that of the shell whitefront. I really ought to get some shell whitefronts, but the silhouettes seem to fill my needs in decoying these best-tasting-of-all geese.

Most shell decoys have detachable heads, which makes them easy to nest, store and carry, one body inside the other. There is a stumpy bit of neck molded into the body, and the hollow neck fits over the stump, some in the feeding position, some resting and some in "sentry" position.

Shell deeks have a metal stake set up which allows you to push the stake into the ground, then position the deek atop it. By leaving the stake out, the bird assumes the resting position, flat on the ground.

In my humble opinion, shell decoys are the best possible choice for the hunter who will hunt many different areas during the season. If that hunter has to transport his deeks in a pickup or station wagon, the shell allows him to carry three or four dozen with ease. They're my first choice. For Canada geese, a couple dozen shells will suffice in 90% of the situations apt to be encountered by the traveling goose hunter. If you are a snow goose hunter, two dozen shells should be supplemented by another three dozen of the simpler, lighter, easier to carry silhouettes. Add a couple wind sock deeks and you are in business.

Silhouettes

Many years ago, when I was but a young sprout, I was sound asleep during a November morning. Outside the snow fell gently over the

Iowa countryside. About ten minutes after six, the telephone rang! Muttering silent curses I answered to hear, "Chuck! I just got off work and on my way home I heard geese! Stopped the car and listened and would you believe it, there's about a thousand honkers on the pond at Weilers Farm. We can't get at them there, that's for sure, but when it comes daybreak, those geese are going out to feed. Got any ideas?"

I told him that I'd meet him at the diner in fifteen minutes and struggled into heavy clothes as fast as I could. Grabbing a twelve gauge off the rack, I made sure that there was a full box of shells in the hunting coat before I went out into the stillness of pre-dawn winter in Iowa. Then, on a hunch, I turned back and grabbed three small camo canvas bags lying on the floor of the garage. I dropped them into the trunk of the car and hurried to meet Eddie at the diner.

Eddie is a policeman; a good one, I hear. He is also a goose hunting maniac—that I had learned from many trips afield. We had made five or six hunts together that year, until it seemed that all of the geese were gone south and it was no use hunting geese which have gone south.

Over steaming cups of black coffee we talked it over. "We've got about fifteen minutes to get set up, way I figure it," Eddie said, "If those are migrants, and they gotta be, they'll be hungry. They'll go to feed early; it being a clear day."

It was only three miles out to where the geese were roosting. We rolled down the window and listened to them, music to our ears. But you can't go on Weilers place to hunt, he simply doesn't like trespassers. We also knew that there would be scant pickings for the geese if they tried to feed on his land. The old man used horse-drawn wagons and picked his own corn, leaving very few kernels in the field. So the geese would be going out to feed—but where? A light breeze blew from the east, and we drove two miles due east. "Might as well take our chances here," said Eddie, "if they don't give us a shot, we'll at least know where they are for the evening hunt."

Encumbered by our heavy clothes, we carried the three sacks out into the field, two hundred yards from where the car was parked in the shelter of a few trees. Working with the speed borne of long practice, we took out three dozen decoys, the cardboard ones, life size, painted realistically on both sides, with a neck and head folded inside the body. As fast as we could force the stakes into the unyielding frozen earth, and unfold heads, we worked to arrange a three dozen deek setup of

Canadas feeding on the cornfield. We took a quick look at our handiwork and found it good. Eddie scurried to a dead furrow, and dropped his camouflaged body to earth. I went fifty yards in the other direction and stretched out with a couple of cornstalks over me and more alongside me.

It was already light in the east, a spreading glory of newborn day. Slowly the chill seeped into our bones, as we knew it would—that's part of waterfowling in the colder climes. Then we heard the excited chatter of the Canadas. They were on the wing and heading into the breeze, but slightly to the north of us.

I heard the high, excited hailing call Eddie sent forth, and I reached for my call to add my invitation. The geese paid no attention at first, then relented and decided to take a look. They came crosswind in a long circle, just as the sun came over the horizon and sidelighted our decoy spread.

Putting my call away, I held as still as one of the frozen clods of good Iowa black dirt that was crunching into my back. "Let Eddie do the work; then it won't be my fault if they don't come."

They swung in two tightening circles, then they were suddenly right over Eddie, and he rose to one knee and began to shoot. I saw one, two, and then three birds drop out of the sky, and my heart sank inside me as the big birds grabbed great wingfulls of air and stood on their tails fighting for altitude and safety.

They didn't all make it. The last two birds were still within range when they passed over me. I dropped the lowest with my first shot, and swung on the second. I drew feathers and the bird slid off to windward, but my last shot dropped him right among the cardboard decoys which had been Judas birds to this great flock.

Three hundred birds flew on to the east, searching for a safe place to feed. We never saw them again, for this was late in the season, and the migration was over.

What's the point of all this? Well, if we had tried to set up conventional shell decoys, or heavier silhouettes, or wind socks, we would have been still working when the geese came over. True, this was a special situation, but the fact remains that the "very portable" cardboard silhouettes have the wonderful advantage of being placed in minutes, without developing hernias carrying them to the field. For "hit and run" hunting, such as we found that Iowa morning, they cannot be beat.

Of course, there are other silhouettes, like the solid plywood or masonite cutouts, with a stake permanently fastened to the deek. Life size and well painted, these artificials do an excellent job. The fact that they are one dimensional doesn't seem to reduce their lure to flying geese. I believe it is important to place these silhouettes a bit farther apart than I place solids or shells, simply because they are one dimensional. If the high flying goose passes over all of them at once, and they all disappear at once, it might bring a question in the mind of the flying goose. But when they are spaced farther apart, only a few disappear from sight (seen from above they are a thin line) at a time, and no harm is done.

There are many refinements on the basic theme of silhouette decoying. How about making up one twice usual size and using it to hide your head when you peek up out of a pit blind? How about using an oversize silhouette mounted on an easel to stand in the water when hunting geese over water? You can stand erect behind the silhouette, even build a shelf on its back side to hold your shells.

If you use silhouettes, you'll want bags to carry them in—either mesh or light canvas, or even burlap (although burlap doesn't last long on this job). Remember to use bags of camouflaged cloth. That way you can use the bags to help conceal yourself when the decoys are in place, or use then to cover a cold wet black Labrador retriever. Even if you don't use it to cover something, the bags themselves will disappear because of the camo.

Magnums

As you will discover from reading other parts of this chapter, I am a firm believer in oversize decoys, usually called magnums. They work exactly the same as do the life size deeks, but they are visible much farther, hence they are effective at a greater range.

How big? Well, I've hunted behind silhouettes that were six feet tall, made of plywood and painted in an approximation of Canada goose colors. This was in Maryland, today's goose hunting capital of the world. They seemed to attract attention at great distances. Yet I am still

This is a good shot of placing oversize goose decoys on a field on the Eastern Shore of Maryland.

wondering whether they would be effective if it had not been for the realistic job of calling done by our guides.

Although I've never tried it, I've seen goose decoys made of painted canvas over a chicken wire skeleton. They were plenty big. The hunter sat inside of them, out of the wind, and watched the approaching geese.

Oversize, magnum and huge—big decoys are here to stay, as long as they work. If you haven't tried the big fellows, you're missing a part of successful goose hunting.

Decoys with Movement

Some fanatics have gone to great lengths to endow their goose decoys with artificial life, either through mechanisms which allow the concealed hunter to pull a string and cause the swimming decoy to "tip up" as if feeding, showing his feathery rear end and "mooning" the oncoming geese. Others simply cause the swimming decoy to move back and forth in the water. One genius of note even has a motorized decoy with a radio control. By mashing the right button he can cause his decoy to swim well away from the others, then come slowly back to the flock. He's not a goose hunter, however; he's a model airplane nut. In fact, I hear he got so interested in tacking his decoy against the wind that he didn't even see a flock of six honkers until it was too late to pick up his gun and shoot.

Is movement advisable? Yes, but it can best be simulated by "flagging", as discussed in Chapter 8.

Decoys that Fly?

Paper kites, painted to resemble flying geese, prove quite effective when the wind is right. Streamed on a short tether to fly over the grounded decoys, these kites simulate movement of birds coming into the decoys, which attracts other birds to come in to the decoys. That's the theory and it works.

Kite decoys are found most often where lesser snow geese are the target. I saw them first on the Lissie Prairie in Texas, and can vouch for their effectiveness. Drawbacks? They don't work when it is windless, and they don't work when it is blowing a real gale.

If possible the kite should be flown in such a way that it is no more than fifteen feet above the decoys. And be careful! I remember one excited young Texan who took deliberate aim and shot the hell out of one of his father's flying decoys.

Windsock Decoys

No one can pinpoint the exact date and hour when the first windsock decoy was tried out. Historically, they have been known to the art of decoying for centuries, but it is only in the last ten years that we have been aware of their potential for modern goose decoying.

What we have here is a very thin, paper-like fabric goose decoy in the shape of an open fronted wind sock. The whole thing, raglike, is hung on the top of a wooden or plastic stake driven in the ground. Atop the stake we place a good plastic goose's head. When the wind is absent,

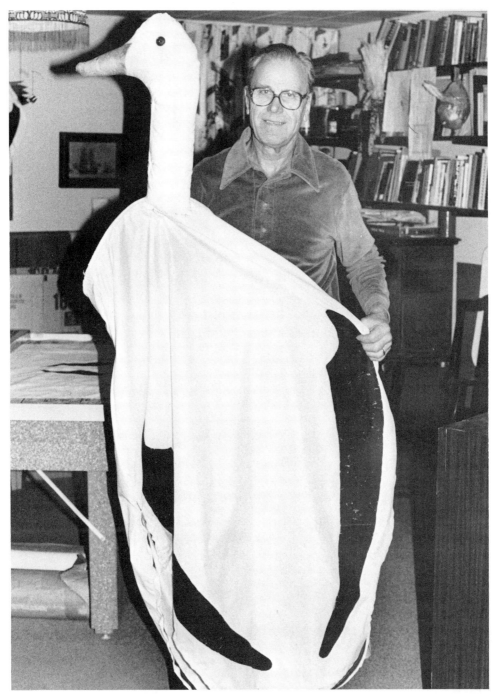

Jelmer Shjeflo of Bismarck, North Dakota with oversized windsock decoy.

the dishrag-like appearance of the inert decoy does not seem to detract from the effectiveness of the decoy. When the wind is light and fitful, the decoy does a good job. It expands with a sudden gust of wind to form a believable body shape. As the wind comes in fits and starts, the decoy inflates, then collapses, inflates and collapses, and the whole operation seen from "flying goose" level is quite good.

How about when the wind blows a gale? Well, I was worried about this. I thought that the decoys might flap an inordinate amount and spoil everything. Not so! When the wind blows hard, the decoy stiffens out solid and does not flap. It simply makes sure that it is facing directly into the wind and it holds its rigid position. Well done for a paper goose!

Seen from the goose blind, the paper decoys (real-life size) seem to be in constant motion. As a tiny breeze stirs them, they seem to raise and flex their wings, then relax into the feeding position. Good.

Remember that the wind sock deeks come in two sizes, life size and about six times life size. The giant birds are remarkably effective in my experience. Like magnum duck solids, these huge imitations of a

This is Jelmer Shjeflo of Bismarck, N.D. who designed the wind sock decoys and patented the idea. He is placing snow goose decoys in a stubblefield, which is a highly effective way to fool snow geese.

goose pull flocks from great distances if they are partnered by some good goose calling. The great disparity in size seemingly has no effect. Remember that, to the flying goose, a very large deek at a distance closely resembles the life size goose close up.

Very large deeks and life size deeks in the same spread? Absolutely. The incongruity of this never seems to penetrate into a goose brain. Sorry about that fellows, but those geese which outwit us all at times are not very bright.

In practical use, there is a way to remove the incongruity of size. Use the giants as point deeks, slightly away from, but still affecting the regular size decoys which are spread out over a considerable territory. The huge birds act as attention-getters, who then come in to the more lifelike life-size ones.

One man who uses the huge snow goose decoys to good advantage tells me that he customarily dresses entirely in white and then sits—in plain sight—between two of the giant snow goose deeks. He figures that in this arrangement he is mistaken for a feeding or resting snow goose. Whatever the method, he says it works.

A spread of oversized windsock decoys serves to pull the geese from great distances.

What goes through the "mind" of a goose when it is seeing the huge decoys below? First of all, he wouldn't have seen the spread at all if it had not been for the biggies. When his brain registers the fact that those are too big to be geese, does he say to himself, "Man, this child is gonna land close to those whoppers. Like an 800 pound gorilla, they can be any place they want to be. I think I'll feed under their protection!"

Ever had the pleasure of watching geese work to your decoys after you've filled the day's bag? Geese work to call and decoy, and land right alongside of the moving, sibilantly-whispering giant paper decoys. They size them up (admiring?) and then they go after the feeding, picking up the corn or soya, or whatever they are filling their craws with at the moment. Once a giant decoy fell over, collapsing entirely within ten feet of a wild gander. The wild bird took a startled quick jump to the side, looked at the chunk of paper and stick on the barren ground, then went right on about his business. The wind sock type of decoy is here to stay. They work!

Mine came from North Wind Goose Decoys, 1107 West Fir Avenue, Fergus Falls, MN 56537. I'm sure there must be other manufacturers, but this is the one I use.

Rubber Tire Decoys

Excellent snow goose decoys (and Canadas for that matter) can be made from old automobile tires. But you'll need to have access to a powerful saw. We want to saw the tires into four segments, each one a quarter of the circumference of the tire. Use this one fourth of a tire for a body and paint it white—with black wing tips if you are a realist. Then saw a simple head and neck out of one inch pine lumber, and paint it all white if you're making a snow goose or the familiar black and white pattern if you are after Canadas.

We used these decoys forty years ago on sandbars along the Missouri River and found them quite effective. Seen from above, the tread pattern simply seems to add texture (or depth) to the picture of a goose. If you have more time than money for decoy acquisition, you may want to try these tire deeks. They are best adapted to use with a permanent blind, for they are heavy and unwieldy to carry.

A spread of deeks on a Missouri River sandbar between Iowa and Nebraska—bodies made from sections of automobile tires.

Closeup of a car tire decoy in use in Nebraska.

Inflatables

In about 1955 I got my hands on some beautiful inflatable rubber Canada goose decoys that were made by a small firm in Nebraska. These birds were accurately painted in non-glare colors. They had molded rubber feet and legs which attached to the body by simply forcing a bent loop of heavy wire inside a collar permanently fastened to the underside of the goose. Stakes protruded from the bottoms of the feet, allowing them to be stuck securely into the ground.

These deeks were easily inflated by blowing with my mouth, and they stood rock steady once placed. The inflatables lasted a long time, for they were made of heavy rubber. Mine finally sprung leaks in sun-rotted rubber and were beyond repair. I don't know of any source for these inflatables as of now.

Closeup of inflatable goose decoys. Note lifelike details such as legs and feet.

100

Taxidermy Geese

A few goose hunting fanatics have gone to the extreme. They've used real Canada geese, mounted by a taxidermist. The only places I have seen this is on the Eastern Shore of Chesapeake Bay, where hunting pressure is very heavy, and it is mighty profitable for the guides to be able to fill the hunters' bag. Some of the very best guides swear by these stuffed birds, claiming that they will work where everything else fails. Frankly, I doubt it. I have never seen any evidence that their pulling power is greater than that of shell decoys, and a controlled experiment to find out seems out of the question.

Militating against the use of the real feather birds are two facts: 1) they are mighty expensive, and 2) they are very fragile. In hunting conditions, it is almost impossible to keep the stuffed birds looking their best over the length of today's season. In my mind, using real mounted birds as decoys is somewhat like the grouse hunter who refuses to use anything but a Parker shotgun. This snobbishness gives him pleasure—he feels that he is hunting the prince of game birds with the prince of shotguns. Okay, whatever turns you on. But a hundred and fifty dollar side by side will kill the grouse just as dead, just as often. I would just as soon have good quality solid body artificial decoys. They'll do the job and last a hundred times as long.

A friend of mine puts out the ideal spread for geese, he thinks; and I may have to agree. He uses six snow geese windsock giants at one end of the spread, the upwind end. If possible, he puts these at the highest point of his spread also. Then he spreads out about 110 blue and snow geese life size shells, each decoy about five or six feet from the other, and all facing into the wind. He has three Canada giants. These are positioned at the other end of the spread, as far from the giant snows as he can get them. Then he intermixes his twelve windsock Canadas with twenty shell Canadas to complete the rig. The general shape of the entire spread is like that of a shallow moon—the kind we used to saw out of the top side of the outhouse. His blind in the near center of the spread, on the inside of the concave moon, is distinguished by three cobs of plastic corn—decoy corn. I asked him if the decoy corn really helped. His answer is classic goosehunter, "I don't know. But it might help and it can't hurt."

Chapter 8

Flagging

Eyes pick out movement! Sounds too basic to mention, but all deerhunters know that they usually spot their deer when it twitches an ear or moves its head. Unsuccessful hunters know that the deer spotted them first—when they moved to brush a fly off their chin, or to scratch an itchy spot. When you are holding perfectly still, most species of wildlife will not see you, even at extremely close range.

When you are trying to decoy geese, you want them to see your spread, but you want them to see it as being perfectly natural. We have all watched flocks of geese on the ground, and we all know that they are almost never still. White geese move around more than the dark species, and the white-cheeked Canadas are perhaps the quietest of all. Yet every few seconds some goose stretches its neck and flaps its wings, as if to relieve the cramps in those powerful wing muscles.

In heavily hunted goose areas the birds are accustomed to seeing large spreads of motionless decoys. Many hunters leave their deeks in the field from the beginning of the season to the end, and seemingly without hurting their chances. It is my belief that geese do not get wary of these permanent spreads of decoys because they simply do not see them!

If the geese do see these big spreads of motionless deeks, they do not think of them as being geese, for they are accustomed to seeing geese moving.

Back in the golden days of waterfowling, hunters imparted motion to their decoy arrangements by adding live decoys. These "Judas" birds not only moved around when wild geese were in the air, they added their own excited honking to invite the wild flock down to get shot. Live decoys added two essentials to the appearance of the decoy set-up. They added movement and sound—and no normal goose flock is without either for very long.

In 1935 live decoys were outlawed, and rightly so, for they were very effective and it was necessary to lengthen the odds against the hunter in this time of drought and very low waterfowl numbers. The ability to use a call became even more important.

But there were other ways of imparting motion. Floating decoys were rigged to strings which could be tugged when wild birds were within visual range, causing them to make ripples as they moved about. It helped, but not much. Some goose hunting addicts even went to mechanical decoys which moved about constantly, adding lifelike motion to the static decoy spread. It helped, but not much.

On windy days, goose hunting addicts used flying decoys—kites which vaguely resembled geese. This worked—a bit more than anything else had worked—but it worked best on blues and snows, least on Canadas. This type of hunting by "flying a kite" reached its zenith on the Lissie Prairie area of Texas where large concentrations of lesser snow geese wintered. But its use was limited to windy days. Which limited hunting too much.

Other addicts used decoys which resembled flying geese when seen from above, on top of long limber stakes, which moved about in the least breeze. These added the required motion to the decoy spread when seen from the flying goose's perspective. This worked a bit better than the kites. But man still did not have the method of imparting motion exactly when motion was wanted.

Some goose hunting genius came up with the idea of flagging.

Lying in a muddy furrow on the Texas Gulf Coast, a hunter is concealed by a length of black tarpaper. He has a hundred white goose full-bodies spread out to lure the geese which are trading back and forth by the thousands, gabbling and honking in the excited manner common to the lesser snow goose. But none of them come near our concealed hunter. Disgusted with his inability to attract the attention of the geese with the call, he takes one of the white decoys and waves it wildly overhead. He does this a few times, then lies back down as a flock of snows swings to his spread, comes in as if on wires and starts to land among the decoys. He fills out that morning by repeating the decoy waving. Later he tells his friends, "I waved the white decoy in plain sight. The geese had to see me—but they came right over to see what the hell was going on. You won't see that many stupid geese again!" Wrong again, fellow!

In a snow-covered field on the Eastern Shore of Chesapeake Bay, hunters got impatient with hiding in their pit blind, calling their hearts out at flock after flock of smart Canadas, geese that had been shot at for five months already and were mighty leery of decoy spreads. One of the hunters took a chunk of black colored cloth and swung it wildly overhead. "Hey, you bastards! Come over here," he said. Amazingly, the geese did. Attracted by the waving piece of black against the snow white background, they "saw" the decoys. A natural looking set up, with the right sounds coming from it, and with natural movement calling attention to it—everything looked right to the wary Canadas and they came in. Goose hunting on the Eastern Shore will never be the same again.

Flagging is now universally accepted as a part of successful goose-hunting. How does it work?

One of the simplest methods of flagging is by using two black nylon flags formed by two foot square pieces of cloth fastened to dowel rods or slim branches. Lay them outside your blind where your hand can grasp them easily. When the geese are within sight, reach out and give the flags a few flips. Make big motions when the birds are at a distance, smaller motions when they come close. The motion—perfectly done—should imitate the stretching wing-flapping movement of a goose on the ground. Don't overdo it.

Evidently snow geese aren't too sophisticated. In Texas they use paper napkins, diapers, even paper plates, just so long as it is something white. Note that hunter is clad entirely in white.

A classical method, seen in Oklahoma where both Canadas and lesser snows were the quarry, consisted of two oversized ping pong paddles, about 15 inches across. One side was painted a bright, but non-glare, white, and the other side was painted a shiny black. The flagger waved both paddles overhead, turning them in his hands so that they presented alternate white and black to the observant goose. It worked like black magic—or maybe black and white magic.

Naturally you don't flag with black flags against black plowing, nor do you use white flags against clean snow background. Remember what your goal is, to make the decoy spread "noticeable" and to simulate the movement of a feeding goose flock. The upward stretch of the neck and head, coupled with a brief unfolding and folding of the wings—that is the motion you want to emulate.

More than thirty years ago a few of us goosehunting addicts conducted some experiments to see just how wary the Canada goose was insofar as decoys are concerned. We used full-bodied inflatable Canada decoys, made by an outfit in western Nebraska. These decoys were very realistically painted, and even had toenails on the molded rubber feet. From two years' experience, we knew that these deeks would bring in Canadas along the Missouri River, between Iowa and Nebraska. We began our experiment by adding a bright red spot, the size of a quarter, to the white cheek area of the decoys. No discernible change was apparent.

So we painted the entire head of the decoy bright orange, instead of its familiar black and white format. No discernible change in the effectiveness of the decoys. They still brought the big birds in. Sorry to prick the bubble, fellows, but geese really aren't too bright. They not only weren't put off by the orange-headed geese, but they actually walked among them and fed among them without taking alarm. A wise old gander should certainly know that something is amiss when confronted with orange-headed geese which do not move, which do not feed, which do not stretch their wings. One would think so, but such was not the case.

We then expanded our research into duck decoys and reached the ultimate in silliness by putting green and red barberpole-striped decoys, shiny white decoys with orange heads, a decoy with the word "fake" lettered on its back in four inch letters—putting all of these bizarre decoys in among a standard spread of cedar blocks. Not only did the ducks continue to come to the spread, but one flock of Canadas came right in and lit among them, stayed for a while, then leisurely got into the air again. Draw your own conclusions. This information, incidentally, was published by Field and Stream magazine back in 1957, along with color pictures of the experiment.

In defense of the goose, let's consider what he is seeing while flying. In the early 1950's part of my job included counting migrating geese along the Missouri River from the Dakotas down into Missouri. I was the observer in a light plane, flown by U.S. Fish and Wildlife Service pilots. This was an ideal way to count geese, but it also gave me an entirely new perspective on what the goose blind looks like to a migrating goose.

First of all, hunters' eyeglasses gleamed like signal mirrors when the hunters looked up at the plane. Surely those same eyeglasses sound the alarm to the goose. Faces also seemed to shine, even deeply tanned faces. This experience taught me to use camouflage on my face, add a brimmed hat which shields my glasses, and most of all, keep my face averted from the goose's eye.

In the plane, flying at 300-500 feet, decoy spreads were almost invisible, even though we were looking for geese! But we never seemed to miss a "grounded" flock of geese! Why? Because there was always movement to catch the eye of the aerial observer. I looked down at literally thousands of decoy spreads which used silhouettes, yet never once was I conscious of the fact that a particular decoy disappeared momentarily as I flew over it. No wonder the geese weren't alerted by the one dimensional quality of the decoys. In flight the split second when the silhouette was one dimensional went by so quickly, and the eye was distracted by other decoys at the same time—that I never saw the deek as one dimensional. Remember, too, that I was inside a plane, without the slipstream to bring tears to my eyes. It is a wonder to me that the goose can see anything more than just blurred outlines when he is flying. Spotting a decoy spread, the goose must make a lot of decisions all at once, which greatly improves the hunter's chances of fooling that goose. But remember, most important of all, it was motion which attracted his eye in the first place.

Flagging is here to stay. Is it for you? Well, remember the old rule, "If it ain't broke, don't fix it." If you are getting the results you want with your present methods, you don't need to change. But I never met a goosehunter who thought he was doing as well as he should be doing. Flagging can improve your chances. Try it! What have you got to lose?

Me? Well, next season I am going to try a pair of checkered flags like they use to give the signals to the racing cars at Indianapolis. Maybe **that** will bring them in.

Chapter 9

Calling Them In

What is the most common result of attempts to call geese into range of the shotgun? More geese are scared away by poor calling than are lured in by good calling.

Why is that? Well, most certainly it is because there are at least one thousand poor callers for every one good caller. For example, I would wager that there are more good callers in the high school in Easton, Maryland, than there are in the eleven western states. This is because the Easton Waterfowl Festival offers wonderful prizes for the winning goose callers, and because these kids grow up with Canada geese all around them all winter long.

The really good caller is a jewel without price, a thing of great value. I have hunted in my home state of New Mexico with George Case, an Albuquerque business man with a passion for hunting Canada geese. Now, **he** can call. I have enjoyed it when he called a passing flock of Canadas from half a mile to the downwind side, had them turn and come straight in to a scanty spread of decoys as if they were on strings. That particular day, four of us limited out on eight pound Canadas. Without him, we would not have fired a shot. A good call does wonders; but please don't forget that a lousy call is almost as bad as firing off roman candles or skyrockets when it comes to scaring off the birds you are trying to entice.

What is a **good** call?

A good call is one which produces the right sound with a minimum of effort. In other words, you don't want a call that you have to blow your lungs out to make the right sound. A good call is one which you can blow softly, or blow loudly, and the reed will produce the same tone. You don't want a call which "breaks" in tone as you increase the volume. Your call must be comfortably big enough. In other words, you want to be able to hold it to your lips with a mittened hand—not a tiny thing that must be held between tip of forefinger and thumb. You want a call which does not change in tone when it gets very cold. You don't want a call whose reed will break if subjected to zero degree temperatures. There are literally hundreds of good calls on the market today.

Get the advice of a "successful" goose caller, follow his advice and buy a good call. Remember that a good Canada goose call is not the best call to use to imitate the sound of the snow goose. If you intend to hunt both species, you'll need two different calls, and your learning job will be twice as big and take twice as long.

First advice to beginners when they ask about calling is one word, "Don't"!

In order to use all the tools of calling and use them correctly, you must **learn** how to talk to geese. First of all, spend as much time as you possibly can listening to Canada geese talk. Don't take a call along, you will frighten the geese. Just listen and try to make the sound back in your throat. Most importantly, try to fix the sound in your mind so that your ear will recognize it when it hears it.

The big goose refuges operated by the U.S. Fish and Wildlife Service are the very best places to listen to geese. To listen to Canada geese, I suggest Seney NWR in Michigan, where you can hear geese all summer long, or to Brigantine or Blackwater on the east coast during fall and winter, to Horicon and Horseshoe Lake in fall and winter.

To listen to snow geese, the very best place would be the Bosque del Apache NWR in New Mexico, where you can get very close to about 60,000 of the blues and snows from October until March. Pea Island on the Carolina coast, Lacassine or Sabine on the Texas-Louisiana Gulf Coast, or Sacramento or Tule Lake in California would also be good. Remember that there are more than 350 national wildlife refuges, and most of them will entertain some species of goose at some part of the year.

Second, get a cassette produced by one of the best callers (more about this later on) and listen to it. Compare the sounds made by your live geese with the sounds produced by one of the best.

Third, practice with your own call so that you can produce the same sound heard on the tape. When you think you have got it, give your abilities the test. Get two tape recorders. Have a friend operate the recorder with the expert cassette on it. Have him broadcast a section of good calling. Then, with the second tape recorder in the record mode, try to imitate what you have just heard. Do this several times. Then play back the tape you have just recorded and see if you sound like the expert.

Fourth, practice!

Fifth, try the tape recorder section again. Keep up this routine of practice and record until you can't find any difference between your sound and his sound. Then you are ready to try it on geese.

Sixth, every so often come back and take a refresher course. You will be surprised at how far from the original your calling will stray in a few weeks' time.

Seventh, every chance you get, go back and listen to Canada geese call.

You want the very best and you are willing to pay for it?

Contact Frankie Heidelbauer, at 2317 East 17th Street, Sioux Falls, SD 57103. Better yet, give him a phone call at area code 605, telephone number 332-4618. Frankie won the world's championship goose calling two years in a row, about 33 years ago. Ever since then, he has been practicing and improving. He also makes the best goose calls I've ever seen, and he makes them one at a time, by hand, with lots of tender loving care and with an eye for top quality.

Warning: Frankie isn't cheap. He has a waiting list of several hundred orders, and he works on that list—when it doesn't interfere with his hunting or fishing. But if you can get him to make a call for you, you'll get an extra bonus. With each call, Frankie will include a cassette tape, made especially for you—no mass production here, either—and this cassette will teach you a lot about how to use your call for the best results.

More than just making the sounds for you to copy, Frankie's instructional cassette goes into such subjects as how to hold the call in your hand, how to place your lips against the call, how to make the sound from your diaphragm, not just from the lungs; the proper timing and rhythm of the calling, when and how to mute the sounds—lots of good "know how" from one who knows how.

The last time I checked, this hand-made call plus hand-made cassette, especially for you, ran about three hundred dollars. But times change, and the demand for his work goes up all the time. So call him first, if you want the best there is.

If you want to try this cassette method of learning, but you can't afford Frankie, "Caruso of callers", here are some others which surely are worth the money, and will certainly teach you how to call geese:

Frankie Heidelbauer, known as the "Caruso of callers" with proof that his calling brings them within range.

This is a good call for snow geese—but not good for Canada geese.

Bob Hester, waterfowl guide and outfitter at Lake Mattamuskett, North Carolina, has a combination offer, a teaching cassette, plus call that I've valued highly.

Dud Faulk, himself a world's champion caller, is located at 616 18th Street, Lake Charles, Louisiana 70601. His calls are some of the best mass-produced calls available, and his instructional cassette is a good one. His prices are very reasonable.

The best place to hear really good Canada goose calling is at the aforementioned Easton (Maryland) Waterfowl Festival which takes place in the first week or so of November each year. Here the callers are hidden from sight of the judges and they blow their hearts out. If you can tell the sound from that of the wild bird, you are a better man than I am.

Remember the old story about the violinist who stopped a New Yorker on the street and asked, "How do you get to Carnegie Hall?"

The New Yorker, himself a musician, answered, "Practice, sir, practice!"

It's the same way with goose calling.

Chapter 10

Blinds

The absolute tops in blinds (in my experience) was used for deer hunting. It was in the hill country of Texas and it was built and used by a wealthy rancher. We sat in cushioned armchairs, watching a well-used deer trail through sliding glass windows. I saw a good looking buck and my host graciously said, "Your shot". After I killed the fine fat little six pointer, the host picked up the telephone and called for one of his hands to come down, pick up the deer, dress it out and hang it in a cool place.

I then opened a beer and sat back to watch him shoot his deer. But he paid little attention to the hunt. When I spotted a truly fine rack moving along the trail I called his attention to it. "Better take this one," I advised. He took a quick look, then went back to the television screen. "Wait till I see if Baylor scores on this drive," he said.

I've never hunted geese in such a blind, and I don't think I want

Some blinds are merely temporary makeshifts, just something to hide you from the incoming goose.

The late L.A. Wilke, well known Texas writer, hunting from a sunken barrel blind.

to. But I tell the story to illustrate the point that a *comfortable* blind will let you do a more intelligent job of hunting. Basically, a blind is anything that hides you from the sharp eyes of the flying goose. Let's look at a few.

On Remington Farms, in Maryland, they use two different kinds of blinds when last I was invited to hunt there. One, they call a "Smitty". It is a simple fiberglass barrel, with a comfortable one man seat molded into it. The barrel is sunk into the ground, so that the top of it is flush with the ground. There's a hinged lid and provision to see out. It works very well when geese are coming in to decoys. It can be put in place in an hour by a strong man with a shovel.

The other blind was an elevated one, raised up to put the hunter eye level above the eight foot tall standing corn. It had a two by twelve plank for a seat and the front of it was made of corn stalks interlaced in a chicken wire frame. It had the advantage of being spacious and comfortable and was well hidden by the standing corn. It worked wonderfully well when placed in a strategic place, such as the flight path of geese going back to the water areas after feeding in the fields.

Blinds are made of almost any material, just so long as the material looks natural in those surroundings. I've hidden under a sheet of tarpaper in black mud fields, under a white piece of canvas in the snow, and under burlap in a stubble field. There have been times when no blind was needed, because the hunter was clothed in camouflage clothing which blended in with the surrounding colors.

Blinds can be very temporary, as when you bend over some cattails and prop up a few weeds in front to form a quickie blind on the edge of a marsh. But some blinds are obviously meant to be permanent. In Quebec, on the shores of the St. Lawrence, I've hunted in a pit blind which was dynamited out of the granite. The bench seat was poured in concrete. Both of these blinds work. They hide the hunter from the incoming goose.

For the traveling goosehunter, a roll of camouflage cloth is a good investment. It's light and very portable. Camouflage cloth will enable the hunter to hide his boat, when it is placed against a neutral background of emergent aquatic plants such as cattails. It also allows the hunter to erect an effective dry-land blind in minutes, in most situations. Remember that camouflage cloth stands out like a sore thumb when backgrounded by glistening white snow.

In body booting (see chapter 15), a decoy on an easel serves as a blind for the hiding hunter. The same situation can be put to your advantage when you try "laying out" in a field. You're wearing camouflage, or are hiding under an appropriately colored sheet. But a silhouette decoy can serve as a mask for your head and face. Use camouflage paint on your face and wear a brimmed hat or cap to keep the sun off of the mirror-like glasses. Keep your face turned downward and peek out from under the brim of the hat or cap—don't let those glasses send a mirror signal to the flying goose.

A blind is anything that conceals the hunter from the goose. **Insofar** as possible, it should be comfortable. This means that you spend a couple of extra hours enlarging a pit blind, so that you can be comfortable in it. If you are cramped and unable to stretch out your legs, circulation will be impaired and it will be almost impossible to keep feet warm. Maybe you might build in room for a catalytic heater? A shelf for shells and thermos? A wooden grill floor to keep feet up out of the water? Build on a lid that can be easily thrown back to let you shoot

Permanent pit blinds are equipped with hinged lids that can be thrown back easily when the hunters come up to shoot.

One of the most complicated and most effective of all blinds is the sink-box type, in use in Pamlico Sound in North Carolina.

unhampered? How about a spring-loaded lid so that the lid really flies out of the way when you pull the handle?

But you must consider comfort in the most primitive of all blinds, also, because comfortable hunters hold still and wait—while "freezing to death" hunters shiver and shake and move about and make bad decisions. Going to be lying out on the frozen ground? Be sure to wear your camouflaged snowmobile suit, and your felt-lined pacs. They'll enable you to "outwait" and outwit the goose, and bring home your game.

If you're going to be wearing waders, better make sure that they are the insulated kind, and wear your insulated underwear under them—for this will enable you to withstand the cold that will seep into your bones otherwise.

Modern goose hunters are blessed. Today's waterfowling clothing is incomparably better than anything available a decade ago. Money spent on "effective" waterflowing clothing is money well spent. With proper care those expensive garments will last you a lifetime of goose hunting—and they'll make you a better, more successful goosehunter.

Chapter 11

Dogs For Goose Hunting

Different hunters look for different qualities in the dog that retrieves their geese. It is how **you** value the different qualities of different breeds which makes them suited, or unsuited, to retrieving your geese.

We were hunting late season Canadas in the Missouri River where it forms the boundary between Iowa and Nebraska 30 years ago. My hunting companion, Jake, owned a "three quarters Chesapeake" with the other one quarter being unnamed dog. As Jake put it, "One of Jody's grandparents was a purebred fence jumper." Jody looked like a Chesapeake, with only a curious tendency of the curly hair to straighten out in patches along his flanks giving away the fact that his pedigree was less than perfect. He was a powerfully built dog with wide chest, muscled shoulders and a short-coupled look about him. His almond eyes surveyed the scene where the hurrying water of the Big

Muddy was carrying chunks of ice as it headed south for the winter. We had decoys on a sandbar and a driftwood blind that had been in place for months and was weathered to the right color. The bitter cold was aggravated by a biting wind. But there were occasional geese in the air and our hopes were high as the sun finally fought its way over the treetops.

In an attempt to "draw" geese, I poured coffee. It worked! A flock of about twenty geese wung past at 100 yards altitude, swerved into the wind and slid down the rushing river of wind to our decoys, great wings cupped and feet reached for the sandbar. At exactly the right minute Jake said, "Take 'em!" and we stood up and swung on the geese. As is so often true when Canadas really want to decoy, they were close in and moving very slowly. We both doubled, dropping four heavy birds—one on the sandbar, one in water so shallow that it grounded and didn't float away. The other two lit in the river and were swept away. Jumping around in front of the blind, Jake called, "Jody!"

The big Chessie sat and Jake gave him the line, a line which would take him well out in front of the fast-moving birds. Jody had his own ideas of how to intercept those geese, however. Wheeling to his right, he ran the length of the sandbar, getting ahead of the floating geese before he plunged into the icy water and swan strongly out to grab the first goose. He returned it—not to land—but just onto the sandbar; then without waiting for a command, he waded the slough between us and the Nebraska bank and ran 200 yards downstream before again entering the water. He intercepted the fast moving goose and brought it to the Nebraska side. Stopping to drop the goose long enough to shake the water off his tight coat, Jody then brought that last goose all the way to the blind, dropped it, and immediately went down the sandbar again to get the goose he had "parked" there momentarily.

Jody then shook himself again and climbed into his place in the blind, out of the wind. I was just saying to myself, "Now, that is a goose dog!" when Jake hissed, "Mark downriver!"

Six Canadas were right down on the water, flying into the teeth of that wind, coming upriver. Unless they swung way over to the Iowa side, they would surely pass within range. Slowly I worked my right hand out of the mitt and let it drop. My finger found the safety and carressed it in anticipation. On they came, slower than molasses flowing down a January pumphandle. At last they were right abeam of us, distant forty yards, paying no attention to our decoys nor to Jake's impassioned calling. Just as we reared up to shooting position, the six geese peeled off to the right, going away from us and picking up speed with the wind. We each sent two hurried shots after them, but only one bird fell. We watched the Canadas disappear downriver, from whence they had come, and saw the one dead bird float into the shallow water of the south end of the sandbar and lodge there. Jody, surprisingly enough, hadn't even looked up at the shooting.

Jake commanded, "Jody!" and the almond eyes looked at him in defiance. That dog had no intention of moving! When Jake called again, the dog growled ominously, a warning rumble coming from deep in that broad chest. Surprised, I almost made the mistake of reaching over to give the dog a shove. Jake was moving toward him when that big Chesapeake launched himself at Jake's throat with a ferocious roar!

That dog meant business! However, there was little he could do against the heavy parka that protected Jake's 280 pounds of bone and muscle. Despite the dog's snarling efforts, Jake was able to pick him up, slam him against the ground and kneel on him. Then he calmly and methodically slapped the hell out of that dog with his mittened hands!

When Jody no longer struggled, Jake jerked him upright and barked, "Sit!"

Jody sat. Waiting till he caught his own breath, Jake then got in position and sent the dog on a line to pick up the downed goose. Jody was off and running with the "Fetch!" Smartly he picked up the bird and brought it back to the blind. There he dropped it with the other geese and nonchalantly resumed his position in the blind.

All this time I hadn't said a word. I was so shocked and surprised by the dog's ferocious attack on his master that I was literally speechless. Regaining my composure and voice, I asked, "What the hell?"

With a big grin, Jake answered, "About once a year, me and Jody have to figure out who is boss. He'll be okay now for the rest of the season."

"I wouldn't keep a dog like that one second," I said, "Why don't you get rid of him?"

"You saw him retrieve that floating double, didn't you?"

"Yes," I answered.

"Well?" asked Jake, "don't you think he's worth keeping?"

My answer would have been, "No, I wouldn't keep him." But no two of us see things quite the same. This story is not told to downgrade the Chesapeake. Far from it. That was the only hard-headed, stubborn Chesapeake I've ever hunted over, no matter what the stereotype is.

Bred for the great distances and rough conditions of the Chesapeake Bay, the Chessie is admirably suited to handling the big job of retrieving a goose which may weigh as much as 15 pounds. If you can get one from real hunting stock, a goose hunter cannot do better than the Chesapeake. This is especially true if you're retrieving will be from large bodies of cold water.

However, the great majority of North American geese are retrieved from land, not from water. That is one of the reasons why the Labrador retriever is now the odds-on choice of 90% of our goose hunters. They can handle cold water—not as well as a Chesapeake, but they handle it without problems and are much more tractable—easily trained and anxious to please. I have a personal preference for the yellow Lab over the black, but that is a small matter. I have two reasons for that feeling. One, the yellow blends into the blind material background better than the black and isn't as visible to the incoming goose. Second, the best retriever of all kinds that I ever met was a yellow. That greatest retriever I've ever met was a yellow labrador owned by Dr. Joe Linduska, and his name was Pete.

I know of a yellow Labrador that jumped into heavy surf on the Atlantic Coast to retrieve a broken-winged goose. His owner yelled to the dog to come back, but the dog probably couldn't hear him over the noise of the wind and the waves. The goose swam away and the dog swam gallantly out to sea after him. Hunting from a permanent blind set on pilings in deep water, there was no way the hunter could go after his dog. He finally succeeded in attracting the attention of commercial fishermen in a passing boat. They took him to shore and he began a daylong search for his dog.

Ten hours later, heartsick and sad, he gave up because of darkness and went home. No one had seen the dog. Later that night he got a call from the Coast Guard. They had picked up his dog. Elated, the owner drove to the Coast Guard Station. His Lab was too tired and stiff to get up, but his tail thumped the floor in welcome. With tears in his eyes the man picked up his dog and started to carry him out to the car. The

Coast Guardsman called him back with the words, "Hey! Don't forget your goose. He had it when we picked him up—almost a mile off shore!"

I've seen Golden Retrievers that made good goose retrievers, and surely these handsome, well-behaved, good dispositioned dogs rate a look. Excellent with children, they make a good family pet when they're not working dogs. They have one drawback, in my wife's mind. They shed a lot of hair if allowed to come inside the house. Not as rugged in cold water as the Labrador, and certainly far behind the Chessie in this regard, they make excellent hunting dogs. It is my personal belief—without scientific backing at all—that a Golden learns his lessons even faster than a Labrador, but that he doesn't retain training as well.

Many other breeds have retrieved geese successfully, but your chances of success are improved if you start with one of these three breeds. One of the most comical things I've ever observed from a goose blind was the sight of a five pound cocker spaniel—a pampered house pet who traveled to the blind in his master's game pocket—trying to retrieve a not-quite-dead Canada goose of seven pounds.

After fifteen minutes of trying to find out how to get a grip on the big bird, the little cocker got a stranglehold on the neck and tugged the bird fifty feet across the stubblefield by backing up. "Don't laugh," his master said," he got the job done." The funniest part of the whole show was when the goose met the cocker with a big "whop" of its good wing. Dealing the little dog a blow which sent him end over end, the Canada started to move away. Undaunted the tiny dog ran under the goose and grabbed it by the leg. That was his mistake. He got pecked and he got wing slapped, but he wouldn't let go until the goose weakened and its head fell to the side. Then the cocker started the business of trying to find the handle.

But you are right, I surely don't recommend the cocker spaniel as a goose retriever. If the choice is left up to me, I'd get a Labrador from hunting stock and have him trained by a professional in the field. When the dog knew his commands to come, to heel, to sit, to stay and knew what I wanted when I said, "Fetch!", then I'd start training with the dog, teaching him hand signals and whistle commands and getting to know my dog and letting him get to know me.

Why have a dog at all?

1) For conservation reasons. The dog will find cripples that you'd never find. He'll be worth his keep in the birds you do not lose.

2) Hunting with a well-trained dog is far more enjoyable. Conversely, a poorly trained dog can sure louse up a hunt.

3) There is a great pleasure in being able to work as a team with your dog, helping him find the downed bird with whistle and hand signals. You maneuver him to the approximate area. Then his choke-bored nose will lead him to the bird. There's a great thrill when this teamwork results in a retrieve. When your dog finally dives into the cover and comes out with the bird and starts running back to you, you'll have the reward of long hours of work. If you do a lot of hunting, a retriever doesn't cost—he pays.

Chapter 12

Mexican Goose Hunting

I do not know of any place in Mexico where goose hunting is one tenth as good as it is on the Eastern Shore of Chesapeake Bay, Maryland. In fact, I can name fifty goose hunting spots in the good old U.S.A. that offer much better goose hunting than any place down south of the border.

Having said that, I can now state that there are many areas in Mexico which offer excellent goose hunting opportunity. Opportunity is the key word here. To start with, there are very few waterfowl hunters in Mexico. Hunting is uncrowded, because the average Mexicano cannot afford shotgun shells, which are not only very expensive, but are hard to come by.

Yes, a hunting license is required to hunt in Mexico, no matter what that fly-by-night outfitter told you. Furthermore, it is a state-by-state license, same as in *los Estados Unidos*, not one license for the entire Republic of Mexico.

Yes, you can take your shotgun into Mexico, but it is a time-consuming business to get the necessary permits and to buy the gun import license. When last I went through this rigamarole, it cost roughly fifty bucks per gun. Many of those who hunt Mexico regularly keep their gun in Mexico. You see, the import license stays with the gun and is valid for as long as the gun exists in Mexico. But if you take it home with you, you buy another one next time you want to take your gun back to Mexico. It quickly gets cheaper to leave your gun—and the permit—with a friend in Mexico.

A combined waterfowl hunt in Old Mexico can be very enjoyable—and you get enough shooting to make it worth while. The combined bag of cranes (those drumsticks are big and delicious), geese and ducks is generous. Combined that gunning opportunity with some fantastic quail and dove shooting and you have the makings of a fine safari for shotgun.

But we are talking geese and only geese.

Canada geese were the first among North American anserine birds to learn that it was not necessary to migrate all the way to Mexico. Canadas are now almost a rarity below the Border.

The lesser snow goose still goes into the northern reaches of the friendly land below the border. Surprisingly, the white phase makes up about 98% of the lesser snows wintering in northern Chihuahua—the blue phase is so rare there as to attract a lot of attention whenever one appears. There are also excellent populations of whitefronts wintering in Mexico.

The northern half of Mexico is an exceedingly dry country. With very few exceptions waterfowl habitat as we know it is simply not present. Notable exceptions are in the irrigated farming country which has developed near the big reservoirs, such as Laguna Bustillos and Presa Halcon in the state of Chihuahua, near the city of Cuauhtemoc, west of Chihuahua City. Here the hunting is almost entirely for the white phase of snow goose, with a nondescript smattering of ducks thrown in. Mallards are mighty scarce.

Another such area is in the country 50 to 100 miles south and southwest of El Paso, Texas. In the vast central area of Mexico, any waterfowl is a stranger.

The situation is different along both coasts, where concentrations of wintering birds are found. Along the Pacific Coast, most shallow lagoons provide wintering habitat for Pacific Brant, for lesser sandhill cranes and a collection of whistlers, squealers and other forms of tree ducks. I specify **shallow** lagoons, because most of the bays opening off of the Sea of Cortez are very deep, with little food for most waterfowl species.

In a few areas near Los Mochis, waterfowl hunting is popular with local and tourist alike, but it features lesser ducks, not the geese we seek. On the Baja Peninsula there are a few great concentrations of brant, but most of them are nearly inaccessible and very lightly gunned, if at all.

Okay, so goose hunting below the border is not good over great areas, but what can you expect if you get into one of the good, small areas? First of all, you can expect smart, wary geese. These birds were shot at when they were only four months old, near James Bay in Canada. They dodged pellets across the Dakotas or eastern Montana, overflew the front range of Colorado's mountains to avoid the hunting pressure, stopped over a weekend in New Mexico, then went on down into Chihuahua. All of that 2,000 miles plus they admired decoy set-ups and listened to hunters trying to sound like a snow goose. They've been to school, and a Mexican goose is a graduate student, believe thee me.

Of course the very light hunting pressure serves to tame him right down again, and by late February—Yes, the season is still open then even in New Mexico—he may have forgotten that hunters and calls are dangerous. But he doesn't seem to lose his fear of decoys. Even very late in the lightly-hunted Mexican season, the snow goose doesn't decoy readily.

Mexican guides and outfitters, as a general rule, know very little about hunting geese. They believe in setting out great spreads of decoys, while telling you that the geese don't come to the deeks. Questioned about this, Pablo told me, "You have to try something, senor!"

The snow geese and whitefronts I'm familiar with in Mexico feed in grain fields. They fly some distance from the roosting lake or lagoon, and seldom feed close to the water itself. This is probably due to the fact that they've already cleaned the near fields by the time I get there.

It is my personal belief that we kill more geese on opening day in Illinois (or Maryland, for that matter) than are killed in the entire season in Mexico. I can't prove it; but no one else can disprove it, so I'll stick my neck out.

Shotgunning in Mexico? Great, but count on quail by the millions and doves by the bucketful to make your day. If you get a kick out of fulvous tree ducks—Mexican whistlers and other such ducks, you'll have fun. But as a place to go goose hunting, I cannot rate it highly. I hope to hunt geese in Chihuahua every winter as long as I'm able—and I don't want you for competition.

Chapter 13

Alaskan Goose Hunting

Christopher Batin is no newcomer to the Alaska hunting scene. As editor of Alaska Outdoors magazine, Chris spends more than 200 days per year in the Alaska outdoors gathering material for books and magazine articles. He is an avid bird collector, and his tally of mounted specimens of game birds now runs over twenty. He is the Alaska editor of the Hunting Report, editions 1 and 2.

Chris started hunting geese at 14 near his hometown of Dayton, Ohio, and has been at it ever since. He regularly writes articles on waterfowling, and is the author of the new book, *Hunting in Alaska; The Complete Guide.*

Chris Batin on Alaskan goose hunting:

Most hunters know Alaska for its big game hunting opportunities, yet few are familiar with its excellent goose hunting. Alaska is to goose hunting what Africa is to big game hunting: wild, awesome and wonderfully adventure-filled. Instead of sharing a lakeshore with a dozen other hunters, you might share it with a ten foot Alaskan brown bear; geese are so numerous at times that you'll hear the din of cackling 24 hours a day. During major migrations, it's not uncommon to observe huge flocks of geese blacken the sky, filling the air with a crescendo of calls sure to excite the most experienced of goose hunters.

The current bag limits attest that these claims are not exaggerated. (While the daily bag limit has been reduced in the past two years, it's still an impressive harvest.) In one day you are allowed to bag a combined total of six whitefronted, snow or Canada geese, two black brant, two emperor geese and up to three sandhill cranes. I can hardly carry a day's bag of geese from the field, not to mention a possession limit from a weekend hunt. Most Alaskan hunters, God love'em, limit their bag rather than bag their limit.

Alaska is also the mainstay of the Pacific Flyway's goose population. Without the breeding marshes abundantly distributed throughout the state, much of the Pacific Flyway would have few geese to hunt. For instance, the Yukon-Kuskokwim Delta of western Alaska produces about 600,000 of the million geese that the state has pro-

Christopher Batin, editor of Alaska Outdoors, is our guest expert on goose hunting in Alaska.

duced annually for the past ten years. About 300,000 geese come from the Interior and North Slope regions and the remainder from the rest of Alaska. Some species of geese are readily recognized by goose hunters, others are more unusual in the eyes of Lower 48 nimrods. Alaska's geese include:

Canadas, six subspecies breed in Alaska. They are the Vancouver, Dusky, Cackler, Lesser (two subspecies) and the Aleutian. The latter is considered a rare and endangered species, and the dusky is making a slow comeback in numbers. The most popular are the cacklers, lessers, and Vancouver subspecies. Alaskan hunters annually take about 7,000 birds.

Black Brant, about 60% of the North American population originates in Alaska. The other 40% come from northwestern Canada. Izembek Lagoon, which is located at the tip of the Alaska Peninsula, is vital to the welfare of this entire population. During their stop-over at Izembek, from mid-September to early November, brant gain several pounds by eating the abundant eelgrass in the Izembek Lagoon. The eelgrass bed in Izembek Lagoon is considered to be the largest in the world, and it fuels the brants' nonstop transoceanic flight to wintering grounds far to the south. In 1970, Alaskan brant numbered 160,000, and their current population is roughly 121,000 birds.

Emperor Goose: Considered by many to be the most elegant goose in North America, the emperor breeds only in Alaska. Ninety-five percent of these birds breed on the outer coast of the Yukon-Kuskokwim Delta, north of Kuskokwim Bay. In the fall, emperors leave the Y-K Delta and concentrate along the Bristol Bay and Alaska Peninsula coastlines. By late November most emperors have left the Alaska Peninsula for their wintering grounds on the Aleutians and the north coast of Kodiak Island. They rarely migrate south of the Aleutians. In 1964, 139,000 emperors were counted on the Y-K Delta. This number has fallen to today's roughly 79,000 birds.

Whitefronted Goose: This species is divided into two different populations—the Arctic and Interior population migrates into Canada and as far south as Mexico. This is the population which accounts for the occasional whitefront taken by goose hunters across the Great Plains states. The Yukon-Kuskokwim population migrates southward to California and a few go on down into Baja California, Mexico.

The retriever guards a nice bag of Emperor and Canada geese, taken at Izembek Lagoon, Alaska.

Although the whitefronts in Alaska numbered as high as 495,000 in 1967, the current count is only 80,000.

Snow Geese: Large numbers of snow geese (as many as 200,000) pass through Alaska's Pilot Point area on the way from their Wrangell Island breeding grounds in Russia's Siberia, down to their central California wintering grounds. A few hundred snow geese nest in Alaska. About 700 of these are harvested each year, mainly on the Y-K Delta and in Cook Inlet.

Alaska's Top Goose Hunting Areas

Cook Inlet ranks Number One as the top goose producer in the state, claiming over 30% of the geese harvested statewide. This is due to the close proximity of the hunting areas to south central Alaska's major cities: Anchorage, Wasilla, Soldotna and Homer. Canada geese are the most frequently harvested birds here, with several thousand taken annually. Some of the top hunting areas that rim Cook Inlet are Palmer Hayflats, Goose Bay, Trading Bay and Susitna Flats. Most of these are saltwater tidal flats.

Biggest problem with hunting Cook Inlet is that it can be dangerous. The upper inlet is heavily laden with glacial silt from nearby glacial rivers. Depending upon where you hunt, this makes walking and hunting difficult at best, dangerous at the worst. Ken Lomax, owner of Air Cushion Guides in Anchorage has been able to solve this problem and keep goose hunters happy. Lomax operates a large hovercraft that's capable of skimming over the mud and silt. "Most of the prime goose hunting areas that we take our hunters to are inaccessible by any other means," says Lomax. "We drop hunters, gear and decoys off right at the blind. We've converted a lot of 'mud marchers' to hovercrafting."

Lomax's goose hunt charters are usually booked solidly every fall. But even without a hovercraft, many hunters have learned how to reach the prime goose hunting spots in Cook Inlet. They adapt quickly to the hazards and—if they are patient—get into some fantastic goose shooting. Hunting methods and means are the same as for hunting any other tidal flats.

Most magnificent of all Alaskan goose hunting areas is the Alaska Peninsula. Traditionally, this area had some of the world's best goose shooting. Prior to 1981, the area was hunted hard by Alaskans and non-residents alike. In 1982, due to declining goose populations, bag and possession limits for the major species were reduced by as much as 75%. The direct result of these restrictive regulations and the indirect result of the public's unwillingness to pay the high costs of goose hunting on the peninsula resulted in a 70% reduction in harvest. After 1982 the hunting pressure shifted away from the Alaskan Peninsula to more accessible areas such as Cook Inlet. As a result, it is now again possible for hunters to experience a true wilderness goose hunt on the Alaskan Peninsula, particularly at Izembek Lagoon. This is currently **the** *place to hunt geese in Alaska, including the magnificent emperor goose.*

My latest goose hunt at Izembek Lagoon gave me the chance to show my uncle, Bob Batin, the joys of Alaskan goose hunting just as he had initiated me into goose hunting in Ohio many years ago. Uncle Bob brought his prize-winning Lab.

Miserable weather greeted us that morning. The Arctic had released a fury of early-winter blasts that beat the shoreline with belts of wind-driven rain, alternating with sleet. Flashlights were necessary to find our way to the blinds and the flashlight's rays showed us fifteen inch brown bear tracks to the left of our blind. Agonizingly slow, dawn fought its way out of the icy night, revealing a wild landscape, miles of rolling desolate tundra, white-capped seas breaking on a uninhabited beach strewn with eelgrass.

Patches of what I thought were "lagoon" took wing and turned into geese. The howling of the wind couldn't hide the familiar sound of goose music—the noise of great flocks of geese.

It was an incredible scene. Tens of thousands of geese rose up slowly in front of us, heavy in the wind. They flew low into the wind, then turned and whirled high with the wind. The Lab was whining with eagerness as he stuck his black snout out of the eelgrass.

Uncle Bob nudged me hard, "Geese at three o'clock . . . and at seven o'clock and at nine o'clock. Take the ones on your right! Now!"

The sky seemed full of Canadas, brant and emperors. I pulled past the largest slate gray and white emperor and crumpled it. My next two shots did nothing but punch holes in the wind. I noticed that Bob had knocked down a Canada and an emperor. The Lab went crashing into the waves, retrieving the birds with the skill of long practice.

An hour later, birds were still streaming past, but our shotguns were leaning against the packs. Magnum hulls colored the drab eelgrass decor of our blind as we poured still another cup of coffee. In the corner of the blind lay four black brant, four lesser Canadas and two of the beautiful emperors. Their white heads and long plume of white that adorned the nape of the neck, along with a body of black-rimmed slate gray feathers mesmerized me with their beauty. We could have had more geese to fill a limit, but we weren't in any hurry. We were content to watch the airborne procession, and only picked up a shotgun when the shot offered was simply too good to pass up.

Emperor geese don't require elaborate set-ups of decoys and error-free calling. Many hunters simply lay out on the tundra and pass shoot the emperors. But the real fun involves the use of decoys on the waterfront at either the Outer Marker or Site, two popular emperor goose hunting locations well-known to those who journey to Izembek in search of this beautiful goose.

I use two types of decoys for Izembek geese: field shells for Canadas, and white plastic trash bags for emperors. Fields shells are best used on the beach, where Canadas like to land and feed on the eelgrass. The plastic trash bags are used to draw in the emperors. Fill them half-full with eelgrass and place them on the beach above the high water mark. Since emperors are curious and relatively unhunted, they'll fly closer to take a good look. Take the shot when they get within range. I've had emperors land on occasion, but this is rare. I remember one time when a flock of emperors came dropping into our decoys—necks down and legs dangling—and I forgot to shoot until it was too late.

Unless you know the area, it is difficult to score at Izembek. Few are more familiar with that area than Ron and Gayle Ozmina of Alaska Goose Guides. With 12 years of experience at Izembek, they guide for custom hunts for emperor, lesser Canada and black brant during the month of October. They offer a complete package that includes guide service, emperor deeks, bird cleaning, dogs and meals and transportation. Price tag is about a thousand bucks for a three day hunt. Ron offers sound advice for hunters wanting to try Izembek. "I strongly recommend good rain gear, very warm clothing, plus hip boots and waders," he says. "The weather here can be very nasty."

There's only one way to reach Izembek. Take a commercial airline from Anchorage to the village of Cold Bay. You can check 60 pounds of gear. Everything over 60 pounds must be sent as excess baggage. I recommend that you send the excess baggage a few days ahead to make sure it's there when you need it. Lodging and meals are available at the Flying Tigers in the village of Cold Bay. Truck rental costs about thirty dollars per day. If you desire to camp near your hunting site, a wind-proof tent and very warm sleeping bag are definitely required.

Izembek geese are not easy to kill. They have thick plumage and as much as two inches of fat beneath their skin from their rich diet of eelgrass. Bring your goose call, for it is fun to call them in even after you've bagged your limit. Brant are different than geese. They seldom fly over land, so you'll need to find a point from which to shoot. But if you get in the right place, there'll be action you'll never forget.

Despite what seems to be an abundance of geese, Alaska's goose populations are in trouble. Native subsistence hunters in Alaska's Yukon-Kuskokwim Delta area have grown in numbers in the past decade, and they have increased their dependency upon nesting and molting geese. The spring hunts for these natives involves more traditional values than it does pure subsistence. They use firearms now, killing as many birds as possible. They also take the eggs, thus destroying next year's game as well as this year's. The abuse of the subsistence hunting regulations is admitted by all game biologists.

It is almost impossible to prosecute these violations. The United States attorney would not prosecute many of the more flagrant violations because the enforcement policy did not adequately define subsistence hunting.

A specific example cited by Eisenhauer in 1977 reported that he observed one party of hunters who collected 657 eggs and 51 geese in one ten hour period. The problem is the same today as it was then. Yet very little has been done to curtail the spring harvest of geese in the 1980's. The result? A total closure on cackling Canada geese and drastic cutbacks on emperors, whitefronts and black brant. Goose populations are getting dangerously low in Alaska at a time when goose

Alaska is to goose hunting what Africa is to big game hunting.

populations in the Lower 48 are increasing by leaps and bounds. While some of the decline in Alaskan populations can be correctly attributed to heavy hunting pressure on a few wintering areas in the Lower 48, many biologists feel that the bulk of the problem lies in the illegal spring subsistence harvest.

Back in 1965, a biologist by the name of King wrote:

"We are deluding ourselves if we continue to say, as has been said in the past, that the waterfowl take by Eskimos is insignificant to the continental picture. The Eskimo population is exploding in Alaska, Greenland and Canada. Waterfowl populations are not enjoying the same prosperity in many cases. It would seem inevitable that the supply of some species of birds may not hold out if the trend continues."

It would seem that curtailment of spring subsistence hunting is required if Pacific Flyway hunting is to be continued into the future.

Alaska is still a mother lode of goose hunting opportunity and goose resources. It's the only place that can offer true wilderness goose hunting in the most spectacular scenery in North America. It's a place where birds still darken the sky; where the only competition is from geese trying to be first into your decoys.

The true sportsman hunting geese in Alaska will remember that the resource is finite, that it is threatened. It's a resource worth fighting for, worth passing on to future generations.

Chapter 14

New Worlds to Enjoy

If you are one of the very fortunate few (very few) who have enjoyed hunting all of the North American geese, there are still new worlds to enjoy. Surely not to conquer, but just to enjoy.

The Grand Slam on North American geese would include:

1. A Canada goose
2. A greater snow goose
3. A lesser snow goose, white phase
4. A lesser snow goose (blue phase)
5. A whitefronted goose
6. A Ross's goose.
7. An emperor goose

Today, I would say that the Ross's goose would be the most difficult to add to the collection. They are never numerous, and they flock with lesser snow geese on the migration paths and on the wintering grounds. Many who have hunted white geese for forty years have never even seen a Ross's goose. In addition, the emperor—found only in Alaska—and the whitefront and Ross's are not available to the eastern seaboard hunter. Travel, my friend. Get out and see the world of geese.

But let's say that you have bagged all seven of these huntable North American geese. Are there new worlds to enjoy? You bet your goose bird, there are.

Europe offers the many subspecies of bean goose, big fellows that weigh in at 5 to 9 pounds. They are important game birds all the way from the British Isles and Scandinavia to the Balkans. While you are in Europe, better try for the greylag goose, which is the ancestor of most of our domestic goose species. This is the bird that Karl Lorenz used to perform his famous research into aggression and bird social structures.

The barnacle goose, breeding in Greenland and in the Soviet Arctic, provides sporty shooting for the hunters in the British Isles and in Scandinavia. This is one of the most beautiful of all geese, in my opinion. On Novaya Zemlya, researchers found that the barnacle geese nested close to nesting peregrine falcons. The aggressive falcons kept the small Arctic foxes away; thus allowing the ground nesting barnacles to bring off their broods. The same strange habit of nesting close to the raptor nest was observed with the red-breasted goose.

Then, too, there's the pink-footed goose, which is shot heavily in Britain and in Denmark. Is there much hunting in Europe? Well, the little country of Denmark annually bags more than 12,000 bean geese, but we can tell you mighty little about other countries and almost nothing about countries behind the Iron Curtain.

Asia has many species of geese, ranging from the spurwinged (*Plectropterus gambensi*) which weighs as much as 22 pounds down to the beautiful bar-headed goose (*Anser indicus*) and the even prettier red breasted goose (*Branta rufficolis*).

That spurwing may be the largest true goose, but geese come in all sizes. Australia, home of so many strange living creatures, offers the cotton pigmy goose, which weighs in at 9 to 12 ounces! Another goose from down under is the Cape Barren goose, a species which evolved in semi-isolation in a distant part of the smallest continent (*Cereopsis novae-hollandiae*). This bird is quite rare, and like our Hawaiian nene, it is semi-terrestrial—but the Cape Barren has lost much of its ability to fly, so I doubt that we can list it as a sport species. In a land where things are not always what they seem—like a fur bearing mammal with webbed feet that has a duck's bill and lays eggs (platypus) we also have the magpie goose—which is maybe not really a goose, but is a "goose-like" bird (*Anseranas semipalmata*).

That bird watcher's paradise known as South America offers some goose hunting, especially in Argentina, where we find the Magellan goose (*Chloefaga picta*) which lives in the extreme southern end of the continent and on the Falkland Islands. Another South American is the Andean goose (*Chloefaga picta*) which weighs in at 6 to 8 pounds. To give you a real surprise, we add the kelp goose (*Chloefaga hybrida*) a five pound goose which exhibits extreme sexual color dimorphism—one half of the pair being almost solid black, the mate almost solid white. Oh yes, we mustn't forget the Orinoco goose, which like almost all other South American geese is essentially non-migratory. The exceptions are the geese from the extreme southern tip and the many sheld-geese.

Many of these geese live to great age—with captive specimens lasting much longer than wild specimens. The magpie goose has been known to reach an age of 26 years, as has the greylag. But our own favorite Canada goose has the record, having endured captivity for 33 years.

Another of our American geese, the Hawaiian nene, has the longest period of incubation, which is another reason for its decline in numbers. The more days the nest needs incubation, the greater the danger from predation and other forms of nest destruction.

Speaking of records, the lesser snow goose has the record for speedy migration, having been proved to make the 1700 mile trip from James Bay to the Gulf Coast in less than 60 hours.

Longest known non-stop migration flight is credited to the black brant which flies over water from Izembek Bay, Alaska to the west coast of Mexico, a distance of 3,000 miles.

Whether you try to meet the black brant at the end of its 3,000 mile flight, go gunning for barnacle geese on the west coast of Britain, or pursue the giant spurwing in Asia, you'll find lots of goose hunting all over the world. But you cannot find a better tasting goose on the dinner table than the whitefront of the western United States. You cannot find a finer trophy than the beautiful emperor goose of Alaska, nor a more sporting opponent than the wily wild-reared and wild-taught Canada goose of North America.

Chapter 15

Body Booting

A very small coterie of devoted goose hunters engage in a weird form of goose hunting on the Susquehanna Flats, at the north end of Chesapeake Bay. You'll soon see why their numbers are few and why the sport is not spreading.

First of all, we must remember that goose hunters will go to any lengths to find a method which will allow them to bag geese under a particular set of circumstances. Looking out over the wide, shallow flats, goose hunters noticed that Canada geese rafted up out there, safe from any hunters. These hunters looked, and drooled. Then came an inspiration!

Why not go out there in the shallow water and stand in that water up to your necks and hold your shotguns up out of the water and then shoot geese? Why not? I'll tell you why not! That water is cold! Outdoor writer Ed Dentry, who indulges in this lunacy, claims that water can't get colder than 32°; so that it really isn't all that cold. He tells me that the upper Bay is strictly fresh water, not salty, even though it is part of the ocean. That's good because brine can be cooled far below 32° without freezing solid.

The wind may carry snowflakes. The wind stirs up whitecaps which break over your eyebrows, splashing your prized scattergun with salt water. Spray hits your beard, freezing it into solid chunks of ice! I thought that the body booter wore a wet suit, similar to that worn by *SCUBA* divers. Not so! The body booter's suit is thin rubber, exactly like waders, except that it has to have arms and a **tight** neck. Under the waders, the body booter wears all the insulated clothing he can carry and all that he can get inside his waders. Insulated snowmobile suits are preferred by many. Ed Dentry says that you also need felt boot liners, and lots of heavy wool clothing. Goose down simply doesn't serve the purpose, as the water pressure compresses the down, robbing it of its air-trapping insulating qualities. Warm clothing is the key to staying alive while body booting. Veterans of this "sport" tell me that the worst thing is that the rising tide puts tremendous pressure on the bladder. Cold seeping into your bones has the effect of making you long for a warm bathroom. There are no zippers on these suits; no relief tubes provided. The result can be excruciating agony, which does not go away as the minutes pass.

Okay, you are a certifiably insane goose hunter and you have your warmest clothes on and you have traveled out onto the cold, choppy Susquehanna Flats. You start out in a big boat, change to a little boat and then wade to reach the preferred spot. You carry a set of silhouette goose decoys, mounted on stakes driven into the bottom sand or mud. You place the decoys in a spread which simulates a gaggle of contented Canadas, burping softly after a meal of Maryland grain. On the back of one of the firmest decoys there is a shelf which holds a box of shells and your shotgun. The shotgun is precariously positioned inches above the water, and you are positioned painfully under the water, your outline hidden by the silhouette deek.

This form of hunting reminds me of big game fishing in the ocean—like trolling for marlin. This form of fishing has been described as hours of unbelievable boredom, punctuated by a few seconds of unbelievable panic. The panic, of course, comes when the marlin strikes the trolled bait. In body booting, it is hours of slow death by

Bill Uphoff of Baltimore rises from behind his stick-up to greet an incoming Canada goose. Part of the excitement of body booting derives from the 360° vision it allows the booters. But guns often freeze up later in the season.

Body booters wait for the geese to fly near the western shore of the Susquehanna Flats, near Havre de Grace. The unique sport originated here as a tradition among duck and goose hunters shortly after sinkboxes were outlawed.

Tom Hartenstine of Charlestown, Maryland, calls geese while hiding behind the silhouette "stick-up" that also serves as a gun rest. Body booters can adjust the height of the stick-ups as tides rise and fall.

freezing, punctuated by seconds of unbelievable panic when the body booter tries to move his cold-stiffened arms to swing a shotgun at incoming geese. Veteran body booter John Simpers, of Havre de Grace, Maryland, says that one of the greatest attractions of this form of hunting is that the geese often come in very low—right down on the water, for they don't expect hunters two miles from land. John ought to know. He's the son of Elmer Simpers, one of three men usually credited with inventing this "sport" in the late 1940's.

According to John Simpers, "I'm a waterman. Pit blinds make me feel hemmed in. This is the way my Dad taught me waterfowling and this is the way I'm going to do it."

Now, do you wonder why this method of goose hunting has not attracted a large following? In the words of veteran body booter Ed Dentry, "There are only about 15 or 20 regulars and many guests— most of whom go once to satisfy their curiosity and never return. But there are no commercial body booting guides."

Anyone who would immerse his carcass in near freezing water for hours on end, risk his life by drowning or the more certain hypothermia, is certifiably insane.

I am planning on trying it this next season, if the body booters will show me how. Wonder how much one of those rubber suits costs, anyway?

And another wild thought just showed up—wonder if this method of ambushing geese would work on the big flocks of lesser snow geese which raft up far out in shallow Laguna Bustillos in Chihuahua, Mexico? Those geese are veterans of five months of dodging hunters by the time they get to Mexico, and they are decoy shy. But they wouldn't expect a hunter out there in the water, quarter of a mile from shore, now would they?

Chapter 16

Families and Migration Paths

In Chapter One we wrote about the many different species and sub-species of wild geese. Next we discussed the "populations" of geese, such as the High-Line Population, or the Tall Grass Prairie Flock. This classification tried to isolate specific groupings of geese according to where they bred and reared their young. Pictured here are the familiar drawings—created by my good friend Bob Hines—showing the rough outlines of the flyways frequented by migratory waterfowl. We use the arbitrary limits of Atlantic, Mississippi, Central and Pacific flyways because we have to have some arrangement for formulating regulations as to hunting seasons and dates.

The instinct of birds is to return to their birthplace when it comes time for them to do their part in continuing the story of their species. We know a lot about "where" geese migrate. We know almost nothing about "why" they migrate as they do. But even without understanding

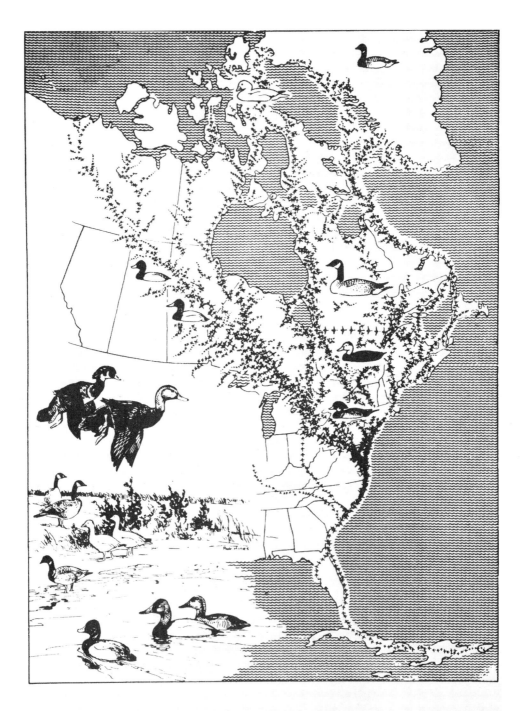

Atlantic Flyway

158

UNITED STATES DEPARTMENT OF THE INTERIOR · FISH AND WILDLIFE SERVICE

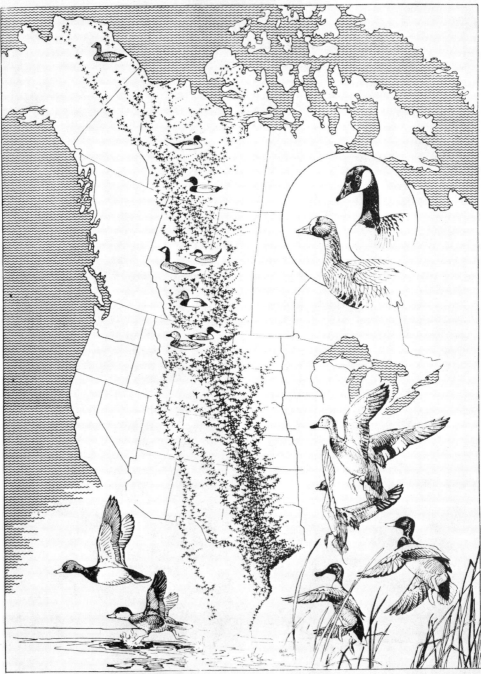

UNITED STATES DEPARTMENT OF THE INTERIOR · FISH AND WILDLIFE SERVICE

INT: 4038-73

UNITED STATES DEPARTMENT OF THE INTERIOR · FISH AND WILDLIFE SERVICE

the "why" of migration routes, we have been able to manipulate these migration routes—sometimes for good and sometimes for bad results to the flocks concerned.

Most of the information we have gained about migration routes of geese comes from leg-banding and the return of those bands by the lucky hunter who killed the banded bird. Most geese are banded on the breeding grounds, usually by being herded into wing wall mesh traps when they are in the flightless stage of their molt. That procedure puts a lot of bands on the legs of young geese, and from this banding we learn that the birds from a certain production area fly to their eventual demise in places many miles to the south. By drawing lines on the map, connecting the spot where the young bird was produced and the place where that bird was shot, we were able to fill in the details of their migration paths.

In other cases, birds were leg-banded on the wintering grounds. This was very successfully done by using nets which were fired out over geese feeding on specially placed bait, by means of a rude set of small cannons. The small cannons, sometimes detonated by shotshell primers, threw heavy weights out over the feeding flock. The weights

Leg-banding of juvenile birds has been our best method to study migration paths of geese. Fish and Wildlife Service photo by Rex Gary Schmidt.

pulled the net with it. Then the biologists pick the geese out of the mesh net, band them—record age and sex and turn them loose. By adding color coded markings, such as naugahyde collars and colored leg bands, we were able to fill in the pattern of migration back to the breeding grounds. Some of the more complicated questions about migration pathways were solved by spraying birds on the wintering grounds with a colored dye, which lasted until the next molt. This produced some results which might have scared some observers onto the temperance wagon—such as bright pink snow geese and blaze orange Canadas. And then consider the psychological shock to the young bird whose mother was pink when he hatched into this world, but whose mother became snow white after the molt!

But get down to basics. A pair of snow geese hatch out a brood way up north in the short summer of Arctic Canada. They succeed in rearing eight young. This forms a family of ten birds. Those ten birds remain together as a family.

That family migrates to the great staging areas on the shores of James and Hudson's Bays. There they form parts of larger groupings, which we then call "populations" as they leave the staging grounds and

Adult geese captured with a cannon net. U.S. Fish and Wildlife Service photo by Earl Craven.

start the long flight southward to the Lissie Prairie (for example) in Texas. They may fly only fifty or a hundred miles per day, if the weather is good, and the feed plenty. They might make the 2,000 mile jump southward in three days, if cold tailwinds propel them along.

These moving "populations" may mix and match with other groupings of snow geese and they may change percentages of blues and snows radically as they flow slowly southward. In general the blue phases will drop out farther north, to winter farther north—while the white phases move on southward. But the shifting between populations is done by families, not by individuals. In other words, an entire family may leave one migrating group and take up with another migrating group. But they will switch as families, not as individuals.

Families will stay together on the wintering grounds. In some cases the young of the year may accompany their parents back northward, again moving as a family.

In other cases the maturing birds seek mates before leaving the wintering areas. These matings permanently break up family groups—which were doomed to dissolve when the parents reach the ancestral nesting grounds anyway—and form into new families as they raise their own broods.

The family group is the strong bond with geese. If you will take the time to put your binoculars on a big flock of geese—even the garrulous, sociable, quarrelsome, noisy snow and blue flocks—you will be able to locate discrete groupings. Study those discrete groupings carefully with your binoculars and you'll find that they are usually composed of two adults and their young of the year.

The importance of this observation of family groupings is that it teaches us why loyalty to ancestral breeding grounds and to ancestral wintering grounds is so strong. It is not simply an inherited trait, but it is taught by example when the young birds are at their most impressionable and most habit retentive stage of development. When a young Canada hatches out in southern Saskatchewan, for example, it is already predestined that he will follow a particular migration path. He will follow his parents. In some cases this means that a goose family from Lake Example will fly across Minnesota and Ohio and on to the southern end of the Delmarva Peninsula and winter on the Blackwater Refuge—while another young goose of the same subspecies, hatched within two hundred yards of him, may follow **his** parents south across

164

eastern Montana, through the Dakotas and down to the Lissie Prairie in Texas. This information was of great importance to those who set the hunting regulations, obviously.

Man has changed goose migration routes greatly, mainly by providing food and water farther north, so that the migration path was greatly shortened—the geese simply did not go on farther south than they needed to go. This is called "shortstopping", and it seems to be fairly permanent. If we improve the southern end of the flyway to be even better than the northern part—the geese will never know it, because they no longer come that far south to see the improvement. Examples?

You've already read about Mattamuskeet, North Carolina, where the geese found improved feed on the eastern shore of Chesapeake Bay and no longer bothered to fly south to Mattamuskeet. Louisiana once hosted a third of a million Canadas that no longer fly far enough south to see Louisiana. They stay farther north where they find plentiful food.

The development of large bodies of water, such as the big impoundments on the Missouri River, have lured many geese (and all waterfowl) to stay farther north where open water is available to them.

Sometimes "home-grown" geese may become very tame, as in these Canadas feeding on the park lawn across from a filling station in Denver, Colorado.

Geese are hardy birds where cold is concerned. Give them open water and food and they don't seem to be affected by the drop in temperature.

The only thing that can be done to restore goose hunting on the southern end of the flyways—after their birds have been shortstopped farther north—is to establish a local population by means of wing-clipped adults which breed and rear young on the southern end. This works sometimes, as witness Wheeler Refuge in Alabama with its success in establishing a new flock which comes to Wheeler each fall. It is being tried in New Mexico with a captive flock of Canadas on the Bosque del Apache Refuge, in an attempt to restore a Canada population which now stops short in Colorado. Sometimes the result is a non-migratory population, which is certainly better than having no geese at all.

Chapter 17

The National Wildlife Refuges

More than 300 areas have been set aside as National Wildlife Refuges, and these refuges play an important part in the life of the North American goose populations.

A few refuges actually produce Canada geese, but their production is not significant in the total picture of goose populations. For example, Seney NWR in Michigan has a fine local nesting population of Canada geese. Exceedingly tame and trusting, these geese will allow you to approach closely and even come to see you to satisfy their curiosity. Bear River Migratory Bird Refuge in Utah had developed a fine nesting population before rising waters from Great Salt Lake inundated that once productive "managed marsh" area, putting an end to the bulk of the goose production. Obviously there are others—and we must not forget that the newly created NWR's in Alaska are home to a very

Canada goose nesting on Seney National Wildlife Refuge in Michigan.

significant portion of North Americas geese during breeding season. See chapter 13.

Other refuges have established wing-clipped resident flocks to produce young which then migrated. Perhaps Wheeler Refuge in Alabama is the prime example of how a migration pattern can be established in this manner.

But America's NWRs come into their own when providing resting habitat during migration and wintering. The Canada goose is the greatest beneficiary of the NWRs safe spaces, but all species winter on these area and all species benefit from them. The list goes on—Bombay Hook, Pea Island, Brigantine on the Atlantic Coast; Horicon, Crab Orchard, Necedah and Upper Mississippi in the center of our nation; Lower Souris, Sand Lake and Lake Andes in the Upper Midwest; Salt Plains, Kirwin, DeSoto Bend, Squaw Creek, Tishomingo, Buffalo Lake and Muleshoe in the lower part of the Central Flyway; and Colusa, Kern, Kesterson, Klamath, Sacramento and Salton Sera in California.

Bosque del Apache NWR in New Mexico has seen its wintering flock change in species composition. While the number of Canadas dropped, due to improved wintering conditions in Colorado to the

Refuge personnel wing-clipping adult Canada geese at Shiawassee Refuge in Michigan.

north, the lesser snow goose numbers on the refuge have grown from about 10,000 up to more than 60,000 in the last few years. Refuges on the Atlantic Coast have hosted increasing numbers of greater snow geese as that population grows to dangerous levels.

The great increase in goose use has posed big problems for the refuge system. At first refuge managers attempted to grow enough food on their areas to feed the migrants enroute. Canada geese seldom fly farther south than they need to in order to ensure a food supply. If there was food enough, the Canadas stayed where the food was, even if that turned out to be Minnesota or the Dakotas where the winters are rough. As the refuge supply of field crops was eaten up, the hungry geese moved out onto surrounding territory. This had two results: It greatly increased the chances that the goose would get shot, and it produced a host of irate farmers who didn't want to see their crops disappear down the gullets of thousands of geese. As a game management agent, I can well remember trying to convince angry farmers that the geese were merely helping to fertilize their fields, and were actually increasing the wheat yield by causing it to stool out more. I failed in that missionary effort more often than I succeeded.

The national wildlife refuges are good places to watch geese. These Canadas at Seney NWR seem to be curious about the author's Coachman motorcoach.

Some refuges tried to get rid of their geese, to push them on down south. They tried hazing them with low-flying airplanes. This was a great sport for the geese, and proved to be very hazardous for the pilot who had to steer a path between flocks of geese, each one of whom could bring down the plane if it hit in the right place. More important, it did not succeed in moving the geese on south. They would not leave the dinner table, once they discovered how nice it was to dine on yellow corn.

Refuge managers began to ask for the privilege of opening parts of the refuge to hunters. They wanted to do this to disperse the geese, to force them to move on, and to lower the very real danger of disease outbreaks in the crowded concentrations of geese. Inasmuch as the policy of the Fish and Wildlife Service had long been to allow hunting wherever it was not proved to be detrimental to the prime objective of the refuge, hunting was permitted. Now most refuges are open to some form of hunting.

Because regulations vary from year to year, it is not possible to give a complete list of National Wildlife Refuges which will allow goose hunting this year. Still, goose hunting is allowed—some years—on parts of the following refuges:

Alabama
 Wheeler
 Eufaula

Arizona
 Lake Havasu
 Cibola
 Imperial

California
 Clear Lake
 Colusa
 Delevan
 Kern
 Kesterson
 Lower Klamath

 Modoc
 Sacramento
 Salton Sea
 San Francisco Bay
 San Luis
 Sutter
 Tule Lake

Colorado
 Alamosa
 Monte Vista
 Browns Park

Delaware
 Bombay Hook
 Prime Hook

Idaho
    Bear Lake
    Camas
    Deer Flat
    Grays Lake
    Kootenai
    Minidoka

Illinois
    Chautaqua
    Crab Orchard
    Mark Twain
    Upper Mississippi

Iowa
    De Soto
    Mark Twain (also in Illinois)
    Upper Mississippi (also in Illinois)

Kansas
    Kirwin
    Quivira

Louisiana
    Bogue Chitto
    Delta
    Lacassine
    Sabine

Maine
    Rachel Carson

Michigan
    Shiawassee

Minnesota
    Tamarac
    Upper Mississippi

Missouri
    Mingo
    Swan Lake

Montana
    Benton Lake
    Bowdoin
    Creedman Coulee
    Hewitt Lake
    Lake Mason
    Lake Thibadeau
    Lee Metcalf
    Red Rocks Lake

Nebraska
    Valentine

Nevada
    Pahranagat
    Ruby Lake

New Jersey
    Barnegat
    Brigantine

New Mexico
    Bitter Lake
    Bosque del Apache
    Las Vegas
    Sevilleta

New York
    Iroquois
    Montezuma

North Carolina
  Cedar Island
  Swanquarter

North Dakota
  J. Clark Salyer
  Lake Alice

Ohio
  Ottawa

Oklahoma
  Sequoyah
  Tishomingo
  Washita

Oregon
  Ankeny
  Baskett Slough
  Cold Springs
  Deer Flat
  Klamath Forest
  Lewis and Clark
  Lower Klamath
  Malheur
  McKay Creek
  Umatilla
  Upper Klamath
  William L. Finley

Pennsylvania
  Erie

South Dakota
  Sand Lake

Tennessee
  Lower Hatchie

Texas
  Anahuac
  Big Boggy
  Brazoria
  McFaddin
  San Bernard
  Texas Point

Utah
  Bear River

Vermont
  Missisquoi

Washington
  Columbia
  Columbian White-tailed Deer
  Conboy
  McNary
  Ridgefield
  Toppenish
  Umatilla
  Willapa

Wyoming
  Pathfinder
  Seedskadee

Remember that the actual areas open to the goose hunter vary from year to year. In every case, the refuge manager should be contacted, well in advance, to learn whether or not that particular refuge will be open this year, whether or not permits are required, and to learn other regulations which may apply.

When we say "other regulations may apply", we are talking about special cases. For an extreme example, consider the case of the Bosque del Apache snow goose hunt. The lesser snow goose population, as mentioned earlier, has grown by leaps and bounds. The refuge is also the winter home of the second largest concentration of whooping cranes in the whole world—the flock that was hatched by Greater Sandhill Cranes on Grey's Lake Refuge in Idaho and which followed their foster parents down to the Bosque to winter in New Mexico's sunshine.

Prospective hunters on the Bosque must pass a special course in waterfowl identification, months before the hunt. They must apply for specific dates. If they are lucky enough to be drawn for the hunt, they must attend another instructional session in the icy cold of pre-dawn on the day of the hunt. They must hunt only in their assigned blind, and they must keep a voice radio (supplied by the refuge) turned on in the blind. If a whooping crane strays anywhere near the hunt area, the voice radio will tell them to stop hunting until an all clear is sounded.

The refuge will provide decoys (you can add your own, if you wish) and will truck the hunters to and from their assigned blinds. Regulated? Yes, it sure is—too much so for most hunters' liking. But it does provide hunting opportunity and helps the overpopulation problem with the lesser snow goose on the Bosque. It also is consistent with refuge policy—to provide recreational hunting opportunity without endangering the refuge objectives.

Yes, the goose hunter is a beneficiary of the National Refuge System. The lands and waters protected by the sign of the flying blue goose are important to the geese, and thus to the goose hunter. Remember that many refuges were purchased with funds derived from the Migratory Bird Hunting Stamp—or as it is incorrectly called the "Duck Stamp". These are funds that came directly from the goose hunter—the sportsman who puts his money where his mouth is by buying the stamp before he hunts.

It is also well to remember that many refuges were purchased with moneys derived from the Pittman-Robertson Federal Aid in Wildlife Restoration excise tax on sporting arms and ammunition. This is a tax sponsored by hunters, pushed through Congress by hunters, and paid by hunters. The hunter pays for most of the work done to perpetuate wildlife species. It is the sportsman who paid for most of the great resurgence in goose numbers in the past twenty years.

In 1987 we celebrate half a century of Pittman-Robertson work. Make sure that your non-hunting friends are reminded that it is the hunter's money which pays for wildlife work.

Chapter 18

The Snows are Turning Blue

When I was a callow youth, the blue goose was a rarity among the migrating thousands of lesser snow geese that flew over the Dakotas each spring and fall. When we did see the "cob-heads", the slate blue gray bodies and white heads, we spoke of them as a separate species. We who were erudite enough to know that scientific nomenclature even existed, we would speak of the blue goose as *Chen carulescens* and the snow goose was *Chen hyperborea*, which translates freely as "the goose from beyond the north wind".

No one had guessed the secret, that these were only two color phases of the same bird. In fact, an Audubon Water Bird guide in my possession, dated 1951, actually has a painting of a "hybrid" between snow and blue goose.

Slowly the obvious became apparent. First of all, it was noticed that the birds were exactly the same size, that they both sported an

Blue phase of the snow goose.

occasional rusty discoloration around the neck and head. Then we noticed that their voice was exactly the same. At first we were confused by their different breeding grounds—crediting the lesser snow to Arctic America and way across to Siberia, while the blue phase bird was known to nest near the northern end of Hudson's Bay.

These birds, coming from (we thought) two separate breeding areas, intermingled on the migration path and on the wintering grounds. Surely, we thought, familiarity attempts breeding, and it is this fraternization on the wintering grounds which has caused the "hybridization" which now seemed to be more and more common. But just when we had ourselves convinced on this score, another factor became apparent.

There was a definite differential in choice of wintering grounds between the snow and the blue. As each year passed, the blue phase birds seemed to be getting lazier and lazier, spending their winters farther and farther north, while the snows continued to overfly most of the nation and winter on the Lissie Prairie of the Texas Gulf Coast, the southern end of the state of New Mexico and down into the Cuauhtemoc area of the state of Chihuahua. Another important segment of the

The farther south you follow them on their migration path, the more white phase and fewer blues you find. Note coyote trying to catch a goose dinner.

snow-blue species wintered in southern California, especially in the Imperial and Central Valleys.

This past winter I had occasion to observe a flock of blue snows wintering in Missouri. These birds were 95% blue and only 5% white. Then I traveled to the Bosque del Apache National Wildlife Refuge in New Mexico. Here along the Rio Grande, the flocks were (by official counts) 96% white and only 4% blue phase!

South and west of the big city of Chihuahua, in old Mexico, there is a wintering population of these birds around Laguna Bustillos and Lago de los Mexicanos. Here the blue phase is so rare that when one is shot it arouses much interest and usually ends up as a mounted specimen.

Okay, so the blue birds are tougher, or their bodies absorb more of the sun's warming rays—in any event, they don't have to take their bodies so far south as do the heat-reflective, warm weather lovers, the snowy white birds. But it is hard to believe that these snow white birds detest the cold, for they chose the wettest, coldest, most inhospitable place in the world in which to spend their summers and rear their young.

In the last few years, some of my friends among the ranks of the federal refuge managers have told me that there is also a differential from east to west, in that the blue birds are more apt to stay east, while the snow white geese are more apt to go farther west. This is certainly borne out along the Rio Grande and into Arizona and California, but I'm not sure about the nationwide picture.

Immature birds are getting to the point where they pose an identification problem. The immature snow phase is duskier—dirty snow color—than its parents. The immature cobhead is apt to have an intricate pattern of light and dark feathers, leading up to the dark body coloration it will sport when adult. But yesterday, while photographing geese on the Bosque del Apache, I had a hard time identifying many young birds. They were dirty snow color, all over the body, but still sported the definite lines of dark on the primaries and across the breast patterns. Will the day come when the intergradation between white and blue color phases will be the norm? Certainly the trend is that way. Definitely the snow goose is turning blue!

In my estimation, this goose is the consummate aviator of all waterfowl. In some years, they leave staging areas on the east and south

shores of Hudson's Bay and vault southward in a series of giant leaps. There have been years when they overflew the two Dakotas entirely, made their first landing in southern Nebraska, along the Platte River, and paused only overnight; then jumped all the way to the south Texas wintering grounds. From Hudson's Bay to Houston in two big flights! Talk about a severe case of jet-lag!

In other years the snows and blues joined forces while still north of the Dakota-Canada border and dawdled along southward together, traveling less than a hundred miles per day on the average. This meant that they stopped near Devils Lake, North Dakota, then near Oakes, North Dakota, then near Sand Lake National Wildlife Refuge in South Dakota, picked corn across the fields near Huron and Mitchell, Lake Andes and Yankton, in South Dakota, then acted the part of tourists along the Missouri River past Sioux City, Onawa, Council Bluffs and down to Plattesmouth, Nebraska. After wading in the inch deep and mile wide river, they took a side trip back east to Forney Lake, in Iowa, just to see if it was ready for them on the northbound trip the next year. The leisurely jaunt went like this all the way to the vicinity of Anahuac National Wildlife Refuge and the big hunting spreads near Eagle Lake and the Lissie Prairie in Texas.

This leisurely migration obviously brought joy to the hearts of white goose hunters along the way, and when they made the lightning dash to the Gulf Coast in a couple of days, the mortality was very much lower than on the leisurely trip. Fortunately for goose hunters, the quick dash is the exception, not the rule.

But I admire their flight ability, not only for the long jumps, but for the aerial acrobatics they seem to love. This exceedingly gregarious bird comes in flocks of 30,000 and up during the northward migration each spring. Courtship flights of three birds—two males courting the same female—are going on all the time, even at ten thousand feet above the earth. When they decide to stop for the night, they often begin a maneuver which I call the oak leaf flip flop, in which they sideslip down from great heights, in sudden sideways drops of as much as two hundred feet at each sliding swoop. As the black wing tips and white bodies come into view in turn, the effect is of a constantly changing black on white panorama. At the same time that the flock members are sideslipping so dramatically, the entire flock is moving like a liquid swirling down a steep-sided funnel, round and around.

The snow goose is a very gregarious bird and often congregates in flocks of up to 100,000 birds.

The process of dropping from five thousand feet to the muddy "hogged over cornfields" below can be accomplished in less than a minute. The birds are not landing because of fatigue. Often the courtship (three-some) flights begin again as soon as the birds touch down after a 500 mile flight.

Blues and snows are never quiet, and the talk of a big flock can be almost deafening at times. But its not only their tongue that is moving constantly. These birds seldom hold still for more than a few seconds. When feeding across a big field, the flock seems to move by a process of leapfrogging, wherein the trailing edge of the flock picks up and over-flies the leading edge of the feeding flock, drops down to earth to feed and is—in turn—overflown by the next trailing edge group. This habit can be put to advantage by the concealed hunter who simply lies still and waits until the birds leapfrog into range. This worked beautifully for me while hunting in the extreme southwestern corner of Iowa. There had been a light snow, part of which had melted. It was easy to crawl down a fence row, get in position and wait for the flock of ten thousand to leapfrog over me. When birds were feeding all around me, I sat up and killed a limit of geese. The tactic worked again the next day in another field about ten miles away.

When their long trip south has just started, these birds respond to a call and decoy readily. It takes them but a very few days to get the idea of what hunting is all about. By the time they reach their winter-ing grounds, they seem to shy away from decoys and don't even hear a call. At Rancho La Estancia in Chihuahua, decoys have almost no pull-ing power. In fact, I think that these postgraduate geese purposely avoid deeks, giving them a very wide berth, indeed.

The voices of blue and snow are identical, higher pitched than the familiar large Canada, and individual birds do not produce a series of sounds, usually contenting themselves with one or two calls. I refer to it as yelping, for they are almost never quiet. In fog, flocks of snows on the ground keep up a continuous chatter to flying birds, acting like they were trying to call them in. And maybe they are, for the snow and blue is a gregarious bird, whose motto seems to be "the more the mer-rier".

Lesser snow goose populations (which includes the blue, of course) are in good shape numerically. In fact, in a few places there are too many snows. A case in point would be the Bosque del Apache National

Wildlife Refuge, in sunny New Mexico along the Rio Grande. Here the population has risen steadily from 20,000 to more than 60,000 despite regulated permit systems of hunting which sought to crop some of the birds right on the refuge. Hunting was only allowed in the feeding fields, to avoid "burning out" the birds from the roosts which were in the marsh areas. The flock continued to grow. In 1985, refuge authorities allowed limited permit hunting right on the marsh area. The purpose was two-fold. They wanted to increase the kill and to move some of the birds off of the refuge into areas where they would be subjected to intensive hunting pressure. It didn't work. These birds are no dummies. They quickly learned exactly where the hunters were and adjusted their daily routine accordingly. They did not get killed in great numbers, and they did not move off of the refuge to any great extent.

Is this change (from snow white bird with black wing tips to a completely different color scheme—blue gray slate bodies with white heads) an evolutionary event? Is the change irreversible? Will the snow goose, as such, disappear from the scene? Frankly, I think so. I think the day will come, long after I have left the goose blind for the last time, when it will not be possible to find the white phase, for it will be dissolved in the growing ocean of blue geese. Vive la cobhead!

Will this changeover to blue then take effect upon the Greater Snow Goose? Will this larger species also turn blue? Surely the same evolutionary influences which are changing the lesser snow will also come to bear on the greater. Or will they?

And how about the tiny white goose? Will the Ross's goose begin to show a blue phase?

Chapter 19

Goose Guides and Outfitters

I have not hunted with **all** of these outfitters and guides.

I am **not** personally recommending these guides and outfitters.

But many of you are looking for places to hunt geese, in a world which holds more people every year and offers less hunting opportunity every year. These names and addresses are intended as a starting place—that's all. They may help you find the best hunting of your life. They may not.

Naturally, any listing such as this must be incomplete. No book could hold all of the names and addresses of goose guides and outfitters. We further recognize that this listing is out of date as soon as we finish it, for new guides enter the work force and others leave it.

When you strike a deal with a guide to go goose hunting, be sure that you both know what the deal is. Spell out all costs to the dude, and spell out what the guide will do and what he will not do. In my case, I make it a point to guarantee that the guide does not shoot. Some guides take it for granted that you want all the help you can get to fill a limit. In my case, that is dead wrong. I'd much rather go home without birds than go home with birds shot for me by a generous guide. Veteran goose hunter Dick Wolff puts his philosophy bluntly, "Tell the guide that he shoots only after the guests (paying) have emptied their guns. Even then, he better not overdo it." It is important to make sure you both understand the ground rules, before you pay your money.

With all of those disclaimers, here is our partial listing of some of the goose guides and goose hunting outfitters you may wish to contact to plan a hunt.

Alberta

Dan Wilson, Hinton, Alberta. Telephone is 403-865-5105. This guide hunts what is probably the second best goose hunting in all of Canada. He is known as a hard worker and is very successful.

California

California requires all guides and outfitters to be licensed. Here are some of those guides:

Donald J. Alexander HCR Box 43001, Alturas, CA 96101. Telephone 916-233-2766

Terry Backer 10041 Scott #10, Whittier, CA 90603. Telephone 213-646-2559

John W. Bartlett 856 South El Molino, Pasadena, CA 91106. Telephone 818-793-4852

Shell Block, Box 386, Tule Lake, CA 96134. Telephone 916-667-5242

Berry C. Bunch 3208 Fairway Drive, Cameron Park, CA 95682. Telephone 916-677-8713

William E. Carpenter, Box 41, New Pine Creek, CA 97635. Telephone 916-946-4188

Joe Cordonier Box 311, Tule Lake, CA 96134. Telephone 916-667-2725

Jeff Cusick Box 96, Orinda, CA 94563. Telephone 415-228-6292

Jeff Davis Box 1027, Cottonwood, CA 96022. Telephone 916-347-6734

William E. Duncan, Box 719, Eureka, CA 96097. Telephone 916-842-5487

Dye Creek Preserve Box 308, Red Bluff, CA 96080. Telephone 916-527-3588

Guy F. Edgell, Box 1179, Burney, CA 96013. Telephone 916-335-2615

Greg Elam, 847 Heath Court, Fairfield, CA 94533. Telephone 707-429-1774

Patrick W. Fee 1315 Dustin Drive #2, Yuba City, CA 95991. Telephone 916-673-4162

Paul Frey Box 2734, Seal Beach, CA 90740. Telephone 213-425-8440

Robert Charles Gilaspie Box 239, Alturas, CA 96101. Telephone 916-233-3173

Harold T. Harper 1189 Weber Way, Sacramento, CA 95822. Telephone 916-447-0108

Donald E. Hay 10300 "O" Street, Live Oak, CA 95953. Telephone 916-695-1977

Dale H. Houston Box 68, Cedarville, CA 96004. Telephone 916-279-6340

Joseph E. Kimsey 5111 Florence Loop, Dunsmuir, CA 96025. Telephone 916-235-2872

John E. Kissel 805 Woodland Park Drive, Mt. Shasta, CA 96067. Telephone 916-926-4365

Keith Kraft 3285 Sharon Avenue, Anderson, CA 96007. Telephone 916-365-0326

Jesse Merle Leighty, Route 4, Box 457, Chico, CA 95926. Telephone 916-343-0519

Bert W. Lemon 3242 San Francisco Avenue, Long Beach, CA 90806. Telephone 213-427-1341

Richard Marcillac Box 582, Redding, CA 96099. Telephone 916-244-1533

Terry A. Marymee Box 68, Fall River Mills, CA 96028. Telephone 916-336-5798

Larry E. Merlo 1939 Durham Dayton Hwy, Durham, CA 95938. Telephone 916-893-4500

Joel D. Metcalf Box 1399, Alturas, CA, 96101. Telephone 916-233-4376

Gary Mullanix 1871 Dean Road, Paradise, CA 95969. Telephone 916-877-7892

Robert M. Norman Box 652, Fall River Mills, CA 96028. Telephone 916-336-6787

Steven Phillips 3380 Pioneer Lane, Redding, CA 96001. Telephone 916-241-4239

James E. Rode 5039 Bidwell Road, Redding, CA 96001. Telephone 916-223-5161

Gary Ross 25405 Teton, El Toro, CA 92630. Telephone 714-770-2400

Ilson W. New 1840 Van Ness Avenue, San Francisco, CA 94109. Telephone 415-433-5812

Arron L. Stewart 4453 Hargrave Avenue, Santa Rosa, CA 95407. Telephone 415-332-5422

Gregroy D. Taylor 24750 Joanne Street, Hayward, CA 94544. Telephone 415-581-2498

William D. Voelker 4221 San Juan Avenue, Fair Oaks, CA 95628. Telephone 916-944-7359

Jim Voges, 818 Park Place, Eureka, CA 96097. Telephone 916-842-3747

Carl L. Zenor 2740 Bradbury Way, Fairfield, CA 94533. Telephone 707-426-1804

In the important goose hunting area around Tule Lake, you may get an up to the minute list of guides, outfitters, meals and lodging opportunities from the Tule Lake Chamber of Commerce, Box 592, Tule Lake, CA. Telephone is 916-667-5178.

Detailed information concerning hunting permits, open areas and hunting on the refuge can be obtained from the Refuge Manager, Klamath Basin NWR, Route 1, Box 592, Tule Lake, CA 96134. Telephone 916-667-2231.

Delaware

M & M Hunting Lodge, Inc. RD #1, Box 67, Road 82 Smyrna, Delaware, 19977. Telephone toll free 800-441-8484. M & M comes well recommended by several experienced goose hunters. In addition to good hunting, they reported good food and good accommodations.

Illinois

The great concentrations of Canada geese in southern Illinois and neighboring Missouri is emphasized by the great number of guides and landowners doing business with goose hunters. Most of these lands are now organized as hunting clubs, or are landowners charging an annual fee, rather than "day shoot" fees. However, many of these clubs can provide middle of the week hunting opportunity at prices equal to or lower than nearby "day shooting" fees.

Roger Dowdy B & K, Miller City, Illinois 62962. Telephone 618-776-5505

Rick Fox, BFR, Miller City, Illinois 62962. Telephone 618-776-5505

Joe Blakemore Blakemore Hunting Club, Olive Branch, Illinois 62969.

Lois M. Farris Farris Hunting Club, Route 3, Box 148, Olive Branch, Illinois 62969.

Doyle Shipley or Gerald Miller Gerald Miller's Hunting Club, Olive Branch, Illinois 62969.

Kenny Masterson, Grace Hunting Club, Miller City, Illinois 62962.

Kenneth Farris Greenley-Farris Hunting Club, Miller City, Illinois 62962. Telephone 618-776-5446

Dr. John T. Schwent Happy Honker Hunting Club, Crystal City MO 63019.

Dr. C.F. Eisenbach Holiday Hunting Club, 202 Kramer, Sikeston, MO 63801.

Greg Patton Horseshoe Farm Hunt Club, Route 1, Miller City, Illinois 62962.

Larry Quattrocchi IMC, Miller City, Illinois 62962. Telephone 618-776-5505.

Gene Fore Lakeside Hunting Club, Route 1, Cache, Illinois 62913.

Ralph T. Lawson Lawson Hunting Club, Box 48, Cache, Illinois 62913. Telephone 901-285-4906

Gerald Clutts Marlin Hunting Club, Route 1, Thebes, Illinois 62990.

Eugene Grace. Miller-Grace, Miller City, Illinois 62962.

Troy Sauerhage Muth's Hunting Club #2, Route 1, Mascoutah, Illinois 62258.

Gene Pecord Oakwood Hunting Club, Cache, Illinois 62913. Telephone 618-734-2698

Greg Patton Patton Hunt Club, Route 1, Miller City, Illinois 62962.

Milton A. Pecord, Pecord Hunting Club, Route 1, Box 85, Cache, Illinois 62913. Telephone 618-776-5125

William H. Hartmann Poor Farm Hunting Club, 218 Wedgewood, Carbondale, Illinois 62901.

Charles H. Emery Honkers Knob, Route 5, Box 206A, Marion, Illinois 62959. Telephone 618-964-1465.

Ivan Miller 1005 Hillcrest Drive, Marion, Illinois 62959. Telephone 618-997-2094

G.W. Harrolle Jake and Norbs Gun Club, Route 2, Marion, Illinois 62959.

Ken J. Samuel Ken's Goose Club, Route 2, Box 220, Carterville, Illinois 62918.

Glenn Lancaster, L & D Goose Club, 1506 Porter Drive, Henderson, KY 42420. Telephone 502-826-4364.

Omer H. Lakeman Lakeman, Young, Ehlers, Route 1, Percy, Illinois 62272.

Paul LeLand LeLands Wolf Creek Hunting Club, Route 3, Carbondale, Illinois 62901. Telephone 618-964-1680

David McIntire Mac's Club, Route 5, Box 81, Marion, Illinois 62959. Telephone 618-993-3349

Gary Roach Walker Club, 1609 Benton St. Johnston City, Illinois 62951. Telephone 618-983-8772

George O. Stout Perrys, Vienna, Illinois 62995. Telephone 618-658-8842

Terry Pike Pike's Hunting Club, Route 5, Box 52, Marion, Illinois 62959. Telephone 618-997-1124

Max Sayers Pinhook Goose Club, Route 1, Industry, Illinois 61440. Telephone 309-254-3304

Jack Sherertz Sherertz Hunting Club, Route 3, Marion, Illinois 62959.

Lois Shoot Shoot's Hunting Club, Box 3565, Marion, Illinois 62959. Telephone 618-993-3306

Ronald Tinges Southern Valley Hunting Club, Route 2, Fairbury, Illinois 61739.

Amos Strobel Strobel Hunting Club, Route 4, Box 29, Marion, Illinois 62959.

Herschel L. Sunley Sunley's Honker, 1804 Whittier, Springfield, Illinois 62706.

Frank Supergan Supergan's Hunting Club, 13227 Green Bay Avenue, Chicago Illinois 60633.

Dwayne Throgmorton Route 5, Box 202, Marion, Illinois 62959. Telephone 618-964-1321

Hugh Cain, B & C Hunt Club, Route 1, Jonesboro, Illinois 62952. Telephone 618-833-7800.

Carlos Brown Brown Hunting Club #1 and #2, Route 2, Box 181B, Jonesboro, Illinois 62952. Telephone 618-833-2096.

James Pickel Clear Creek Club, Route 1, Jonesboro, Illinois 62952. Telephone 618-833-5989

Bill Davis Davis Farms Hunting Club, Route 1, McClure, Illinois 62957. Telephone 618-833-2488

Collin Cain Grassy Lake Hunting Club, Route 2, Jonesboro, Illinois 62952. Telephone 618-833-7890

Morris Foster Hoppy's Flyway, Route 2, Jonesboro, Illinois 62952.

Irvin E. Fuchs Lyerla Lake Farms, McClure, Illinois 62957. Telephone 618-833-5900

George R. Weeks Many Ponds Farm, Route 1, Box 391, McClure, Illinois 62957. Telephone 314-335-8361

Paul Morgan Run-n-Lake, Jonesboro, Illinois 62952. Telephone 618-833-2679

Ted L. Valentine Sunrise Hunting Club, 226 E. Field Drive, Red Bud, Illinois 62278. Telephone 618-282-3113

Darrell Ury Ury's Flyway Club, Box P, Jonesboro, Illinois 62952.

Robert Sauerbrun S & R, Miller City, Illinois 62962. Telephone 618-776-5505

Charles Bonifield STB, Miller City, Illinois 62962. Telephone 618-776-5505

C.J. & J.B. Worthington, Shasta, Cache, Illinois 62913.

Clayton Sondag Sondag Chevy, Miller City, Illinois 62962.

Peggy Shipley Sunset Hunting Club, Box 205, Olive Branch, Illinois 62969.

Tim Simmon T & S, Miller City, Illinois 62962.

Harold Burgard Willis Hunter's Haven, Freeburg, Illinois 62243.

Chesley Willis Willis Hunting Club, Route 1, Cache, Illinois 62913. Telephone 618-776-5551

David Willis Willis & Oehler Hunting Club, Miller City, Illinois 62962.

E. Allan Hicks Alan's Hunting Club, Route 1, Box 15M, Freeburg, Illinois 62243.

Paul Bush Bush Hunt Club, Route 3, Carbondale, Illinois 62901. Telephone 618-964-1382

Marshall Morgan 1225 S. Court, Marion, Illinois 62959.

Robert Ceder Ceder's Goose Club, 6303 Martin Court, Willowbrook, Illinois 60521.

Alfred Fluck Country Kitchen Hunting Club, Route 6, Box 647, Marion, Illinois 62959. Telephone 618-997-2697

Mark Schaede D & M Hunting Club #1 and #2, Marion, Illinois 62959. Telephone 618-993- 6011

Donald L. Hagan Don Hagan Goose Club, Route 1, Box 69, Lenzburg, Illinois 62255. Telephone 618-475-3653

Don C. Hawthorne Don C. Hawthorne Club, Route 1, DeSoto, Illinois 62924. Telephone 618-457-5170

Jack Edwards E & K, 513 S. Court, Marion, Illinois 62959. Telephone 618-993-3019

Elwyn Collins, Jr. Fox's Estate, Route 2, Creal Springs, Illinois 62922.

Ethel Hawthorne Ethel Hawthorne Club, Route 1, DeSoto, Illinois 62924. Telephone 618-457-5170

Laverne Ferrell Ferrell's Hunting Club, Route 3, Box 14, Carterville, Illinois 62918. Telephone 618-985-4561

Craig Wubben Route 1, Box 172, Manito, Illinois 61546. Telephone 618-968-7063

Donald Wallace Grafton Hunting Club, Grafton, Illinois 62037. Telephone 618-687-2690

Charles Eichorn Gray Duck Lodge, 2013 Nave, Metropolis, Illinois 62960.

Laverne Fosse Green Acres Goose Club, Route 3, Box 34A, Marion, Illinois 62959.

Fred D. Nolen Happy Hollow, 13 Pinewood Drive, Carbondale, Illinois 62901.

Don R. Lucas Honker Hill, Inc. Box 387, West Frankfort, Illinois 62896. Telephone 618-932-3322

Charles Heyde Honkers Haven, 1812 Juliane Drive, Marion, Illinois 62959.

Maryland

Bill Perry, well-known outdoor writer from Royal Oak, MD, recommends these three guides in the wonderful goose hunting area known as the Eastern Shore.

Floyd Price c/o Vonnie's Sporting Goods, Kennedyville, MD 21645. Telephone 301-778-5300, ask for Miss Kay.

S.W. (Hoss) Delahay, Jr. Trappe, MD 21673. Telephone 301-476-3126.

Novak-Higgins Route 1, Box 817, St. Michaels, MD 21663. Telephone 301-745-2844.

Lee Peters, 1805 Trout Farm Road, Jarrettsville, MD 21084. Telephone 301-557-8068

That's the end of Bill Perry's recommendations. Now—there are at least 125 licensed goose hunting guides in the great goose state of Maryland. For a complete, up to date list, please contact Francis X. Kelly, Division of Tourist Development, 45 Calvert Street, Annapolis, MD 21401. Frank's telephone number is 301-269-3517. Believe thee me, there is no shortage of goose hunting opportunity in Maryland—especially on the Eastern Shore of Chesapeake Bay, one of America's most valuable estuaries.

Missouri

The snow and blue goose hunting near Squaw Creek National Wildlife Refuge in northwestern Missouri ranks as some of the best in the nation.

Landowners near the refuge sell the goose hunting privilege on their land. Here are four of these landowners and their telephone numbers, to assist you in lining up a hunt.

Dorothy Dodson 816-442-3897
Sportsman's Lodge, Georgia Stone 816-442-7508
Niel Houser 816-453-0505
Stan and Jim 816-238-3655

Note that the Missouri Department of Conservation owns the Bob Brown Wildlife Area, only three miles south of the Squaw Creek refuge. This 2500 acre property is open to walk in hunting of geese. On the Bob Brown, all hunting stops at one p.m. to allow the waterfowl a bit of peace and quiet.

There's excellent hunting for Canada geese near the Swan Lake National Wildlife Refuge in Missouri. It's near the town of Chillicothe, if you're looking for it on the map. Landowners surrounding the refuge rent out their pit blinds at a reasonable rate. Here are some of them:

John Dougherty Sumner, MO 64681. Telephone 816-856-3560
Floyd Thronsberry "Gumbo Acres", Sumner, MO 64681. Telephone 816-856-3368
Dick Ponting Hale, MO 64653. Telephone 816-565-2224
George Duncan Route 1, Hale, MO 64653. Telephone 816-565-2245
Bill Wilson 904 Meade Street, Brookfield, MO 64628. Telephone 816-258-2196 or 816-256-3221
Charles Kaye Sumner, MO 64681. Telephone 816-856-3381 or 816-856-3325
George Yokel Sumner, MO 64681. Telephone 816-856-3301
Sum Goose Club Box 30A, Sumner, MO 64681. Telephone is 816-856-3348
W.T. Stewart Sumner, MO 64681. Telephone is 816-856-3597
E.L. Reed Reeds Seeds, Chillicothe, MO 64601. Telephone 816-646-4426
William Montgomery Route 1, Box 55, Sumner, MO 64681. Telephone is 816-856-3395
Raymond Brown Mendon, MO 64660. Telephone is 816-272-3859
Greg Dougherty Route 1, Box 296A, Hale, MO 64653. Telephone is 816-565-2249
Chet Smith Mendon, MO 64660. Telephone is 816-272-3385

North Carolina

In North Carolina, the law requires that guides be licensed, but it does not require that landowners who lease goose hunting privileges be licensed.

Outer Banks Waterfowl (blinds from Currituck to Oregon Inlet). 67 East Dogwood Trail, Kitty Hawk, NC 27949. Telephone 919-261-2454. Mostly snow goose hunting.

James Hasty Outer Banks Outdoors Limited, P.O. Box 939, Nags Head, NC 27959 Telephone 919-441-7656. Mostly snow goose hunting.

Captain Arvin Midgett, Manteo, NC 27954. Mostly snow geese. We've never hunted with Captain Midgett, but we have fished with him, as he operates a charter boat offshore. Good man.

Bob Hester Hester's Mattamuskeet Inn, Route 1, Box 1b, Fairfield, NC 27826, mostly Canada goose hunting. We know Bob. He's an expert goose caller. Telephone 919-926-3021 or 926-4851

Feather and Fin Inn Fairfield, NC 27826. Telephone 919-926-8101. Mostly Canada goose hunting.

Pamlico Manor, P.O. Box 227, Engelhard, NC 27824. Telephone 919-925-6161. Mostly Canada goose hunting.

Jeffrey and Rodney Berry. I have only a telephone number for this pair. It's 919-925-7901 between seven and ten p.m., and 919-926-3411 any time. Mostly Canada goose hunting.

Jamin Simmons Rt. #1, Box 81-A1, Fairfield, NC. 27826, Telephone 919-926-2891. Mostly Canada goose hunting.

Saskatchewan

BRETT POWELL Box 1, Swift Current, Saskatchewan. His telephone number is 306-773-9793. He lives in Cantaur, on the edge of prime goose hunting country. Born in the area, he knows every farmer for miles around. He has his own pit digging machine and is able to place pits in the right locations. This guide can put you onto geese in the morning and provide excellent upland game bird hunting in the afternoon.

A successful hunt in South Dakota.

South Dakota

DAKOTA DREAM HUNTS Route 2, Box 534, Arlington, S.D. 57212. Telephone is 605-983-3291

Texas

The first four listings in the Magnificent Empire of Texas are well recommended, indeed. Dan Klepper, long time outdoor editor for the San Antonio News Express, and a close personal friend of mine, has hunted with these four, and says that they are good. What higher recommendation could there be?

Marvin's Blue Goose Hunting Club (Eagle Lake-Altair) Full service goose hunting on rice prairies, lodging, meals and bird processing available. Minimum party of four. Telephone John Fields at 409-234-3597.

Jimmy Reel Goose Hunting Club (Eagle Lake, Lissie, Garwood) Full service goose hunts on rice prairies. Call Bill Appelt at 409-234-3808

Clifton Tyler Hunting Club (Eagle Lake Garwood) Full Service Goose hunts on rice prairies. Minimum party of four, lodging available. Call 409-732-6502

Arthur B. and Dick Hudgins Hunting Club (Hungerford) Goose hunts on rice prairies, with pit blinds and full-bodied decoys furnished (no guides) breakfast and bird processing available. Call 409-532-3198.

In addition to these recommended by Dan Klepper from personal experience, there are many other goose hunting opportunities in Texas. Here are some of them:

MARK STEPHENS (Katy-Brookshire) Full service goose hunts on rice prairies. Call 409-578-8146

WILDFOWLERS (Katy-Brookshire-Eagle Lake) Full service hunts on rice prairies. Call Keith McCoy at 409-341-7323

KATY HUNTING CLUB Full service goose hunts on rice prairies and reservoirs. Call Doug at 409-468-7788

TEXAS SAFARIS (Katy-Brookshire) Goose hunts on rice prairies. Call Lyle Jordan at 409-391-7232

THE FEATHER MERCHANTS (El Campo-Speaks-Palacios) Full service goose hunts on rice prairies and ponds. Lodging meals and bird processing available. Call Dave Jenkins at 512-798-4707

GULF COAST HUNTING Goose hunting in rice area. Call Gary Sanders at 409-431-0464

AUSTIN COUNTY DUCK CLUB (Eagle Lake-Sealey-Wallis) Full service goose hunts on rice prairies. Call 409-478-6391

TEXAS RICE BELT HUNTING CLUB (Garwood) Full service goose hunts on rice prairies. Heated blinds! Lodging, meals and bird processing available. Call David Ordonez at 409-729-7259

DOUBLE L HUNTING CLUB (Garwood) Full service goose hunts on rice prairie. Unguided, walk in hunts available. Call Chris Labay at 409-758-3615

ATTWATER GUIDE SERVICE (West Galveston Bay) Full service goose hunting on marsh ponds and rice fields with transportation to blinds if needed. Call Buck Applewhite at 409-488-2911

PINTAIL HUNTING CLUB (El Campo) Full service goose hunts on rice prairies and reservoirs. Package hunts with lodging, three meals and bird processing available. Call Al Shimek at 409-732-6917

Waterfowl Specialties (El Campo) Full service goose hunts on rice prairies. Bird processing available. Call Terry Karstedt at 409-543-1109

WILD GOOSE HUNTING CLUB (El Campo) Full service goose hunts on rice prairies. Call Pat Johnson at 409-5434-8587

GADEKE BROTHERS HUNTING (El Campo) Full service goose hunts on rice prairies. Call Billy Gadeke at 409-543-2859

WETLANDS HUNTING CLUB (El Campo) Full service goose hunting on rice prairies and ponds. Lodging, meals and processing available. Call Pat Norton at 409-543-5236

A WATERFOWLERS DREAM (Port O'Connor-Port Lavaca) Full service goose hunts on marsh ponds, rice fields, and bay flats. Call James Bone at 512-470-1196

CLUB LA CAZA (Collegeport-East Palacios Bay) Full service goose hunts on rice prairies and ponds. Lodging and meals available. Call Will Fisher at 409-956-7106

JIMMY GODDARD GUIDE SERVICE (Winnie-Devers) Full service goose hunts on rice and soybeans. Call Jimmy Goddard at 409-453-6610

LOS PATOS GUIDE SERVICE Full service goose hunts on marsh ponds, rice prairies, and reservoirs. Lodging and air boat transportation available. Call Forrest West at 409-286-5767

LAGOW LODGE (Anahuac) Full service goose hunts on marsh ponds rice prairies and reservoirs. Transportation to marsh blinds furnished, lodging available. Call Gene Campbell at 409-424-7589

LOS GANSOS (East Galveston Bay) Full service goose hunts, lodging meals and processing available. Call Sonny Baughman at 409-355-2342

GREENHEAD GUIDE SERVICE (Anahuac) Full service goose hunts. Lodging, meals and processing available. Call Jack Holland at 409-646-31237

EAST BAY HUNTING LODGE (Anahuac) Package hunts for geese. Everything included. Call Jesse Dee Leggett at 409-252-3201

MARSHLAND GUIDE SERVICE (Anahuac) Full service goose-hunts on marsh ponds and bay flats. Call Jeff Charron at 409-896-0420

EARL SANDERS (Anahuac) Full service goose hunts on rice prairies. Call Earl at 409-682-1837.

RICHARD PRO'S GUIDE SERVICE (Huffman-Dayton) Full service goose hunting on rice prairies. Call Richard Prochazka at 409-324-3017

BUTCH WAGGONER (Katy-Brookshire) Full service goose hunts on rice prairies. Call 409-391-4381

OUTDOOR HERITAGE (Katy-Brookshire) Full service goose hunting on rice prairies. Call Gary Cahill at 409-391-2400.

CARL HOPKINS (Katy-Brookshire) Full service goose hunts on rice prairies. Call 409-391-0945

KEITH HOPKINS (Katy-Brookshire) Full service goose hunts on rice prairies. Call 409-391-6381

KATY PRAIRIE OUTFITTERS (Katy-Brookshire-Hockley-Eagle Lake) Full service goose hunts on rice country. Call Larry Gore at 409-495-2862

RANDY TRIPLETT (Katy-Brookshire) Full service goose hunts on rice country. Call 4509-391-9332

SCOOTER McMEANS (Katy) Full service goose hunting on rice country. Also walk in hunting with nothing furnished. Call 409-391-2319

MIKE WRIGHT (Katy) Full service goose hunts on rice country. Call 409-391-7149 after six p.m.

CHRIS LUCCI Full service goose hunts on rice prairies. Call 409-467-0856

ED KEY (Katy-Brookshire) Full service goose hunts on rice country. Call 4509-376-1533.

Virginia

PIEDMONT GUIDES AND GUNNERS Route 2, Box 12, Louisa, VA 23093. Telephone is 703-967-0810

Capt. Ray Shepherd, P.O. Box 47, Morattico, VA 22523. Telephone is 804-462-7149.

Note that both of these Virginia listings are on the western shore of Chesapeake Bay. There are more guides and better goose hunting on the eastern shore of the Bay, but still in Virginia.

Chapter 20

Clothing for Goose Hunters

From the moment I lay down on the flint-hard frozen ground near Ute Lake in eastern New Mexico, I knew it was a mistake. As I pulled the camouflage netting over me and laid my gun across my body, I knew I wasn't going to be able to handle the cold.

That's quite an admission, coming from one who was born and raised in North Dakota and who had enjoyed hunting in sub-zero weather in that prairie state. The high, thin air of New Mexico was cold that morning, and the wind whistled across that brown dirt stubblefield with a fury that ripped body heat away from my old carcass. My son Dan and his friend, Frank Bush, were hidden beneath similar sheets of camo netting. Fifty silhouette decoys nodded in the wind, and even they looked cold. We had fifteen minutes to go to legal shooting time, and probably an hour or two before the big flock of Canadas roosting on the lake would fly out to feed.

Browning makes this excellent parka within a parka which insulates me against the worst cold in the goose blind.

There wasn't a sound out of any one of us for the first quarter hour. We were too cold to talk, and we scrounched down against the frigid earth, seeking non-existent warmth. Gradually the cold seeped in. Slowly the truth dawned on me. I was not dressed warmly enough. I wore canvas hunting pants over insulated underwear, a heavy wool sweater under a hooded parka, and heavy wool socks inside of loose fitting leather boots. The feet were the first to go. Leather is a lousy insulator and the frost found an entrance. Then the cold crept up through my bones, and I started shivering and chattering my teeth— not voluntarily. I couldn't stop! When my teeth were chattering so bad that I worried about chipping the enamel, I rolled over on one elbow to survey the scene. Frank's voice came softly from under the camo, "Danny, tell me again that part about how much fun I'm having."

That's when I said, "Sorry, men, but I've enjoyed about all of this that I can stand. I'll meet you back at the truck." I got out of sight as fast as my cold-stiffened body would move, and took refuge inside the cab of my old Dodge truck. There the heater slowly brought sensation back into my feet, my hands were able to uncurl, and I stopped shivering. I shed the parka in half an hour.

Warmed and comfortable, I nodded off to sleep. My dreams were interrupted by the distant thudding of shotguns, and I looked back at the field in time to see three hundred honkers lift up and go off to the east. I put the glasses on the scene and watched Frank and Dan each pick up two big honkers.

Now, I'll grant you that they were younger and tougher than me. But that was not the difference. They were wearing snowmobile suits over insulated underwear. Their feet were inside felt-lined pacs, their hands encased in big bulky mittens and their heads covered with down-filled caps which included earflaps tied under the chin. Because they were properly clothed, they could take it where I couldn't, and they were rewarded with four eight pound honkers.

Since that day I've given up the belief that New Mexico is far enough south so that I don't need to dress for cold. Early mornings in the high land can be mighty cold, even as far south as this. In fact, we dress every bit as warmly when we hunt snow geese in the Mexican state of Chihuahua—and believe me, there are times when we need it all.

If you intend to wield a shotgun with deadly effect, you have to be comfortable. If you want to wield a shotgun with deadly effect, you have to be able to move freely. Therein lies the problem. If you "layer up" enough clothing to be warm, you are about as agile as a hippo, and twice as slow moving. Your clothing must stop the wind, but it cannot be air tight (like rubberized cloth), for that will not let the perspiration escape. A damp hunter is going to be a cold hunter, no matter how many clothes he wears. The principle of "layering"—putting on more layers to keep warm—works both ways. You can also remove clothing a layer at a time when it warms up. In the goose blind, it is not unusual to encounter temperatures near zero in the early bright, and still have 55° by noon of a sunny day.

I'd like to nominate some clothing which has proved its worth to me in the goose blind. If it is moderately cold (like the weather that is usually encountered in Maryland, on the Eastern Shore of the Bay) I am well served by the coverall made by Columbia Sporting Goods, of Portland, Oregon. It is insulated well, and the outer shell is *Gore-Tex*. Very important to me, it has lots of good pockets, big enough to be worthwhile, and all closed with effective *Velcro* closures so that you

Goose hunter dresses in white to hide among his snow goose decoys.

can open and close them with mittens on your hands. Equally important, there are well-fitted *Velcro* closures at the wrists which prevent the cold breezes from working up the sleeve. The sleeve is big enough to wear a full length glove or mitten inside of it, and still snug the *Velcro* fastener up tight when your gloved wrist is back inside the sleeve. A knitted collar makes an efficient closure around the neck, helping you trap body heat within. Zippers extend from knee to ankle, which makes it much easier to don the garment over heavier clothes, if need be. The outer shell is *Gore-Tex*, and that deserves a word or two. A man named W.L. Gore researched possible new uses for the DuPont material known as *Teflon*. You know *Teflon* as the non-stick stuff which lines the frying pan so that your fried eggs will slip out of the pan easily, instead of sticking. Well, Mr. Gore found out that *Teflon* could be manufactured with millions of incredibly small holes per square inch. This stuff would allow air to move through it, but would not allow drops of moisture to move through—the tiny holes simply were too small for the smallest droplets of water. The implications for sportsman's clothings were immediately evident. It provides the outer shell for my favorite goose hunting coverall, among a million other uses.

On the many occasions when it is too cold for this all purpose coverall, I go to the much heavier snowmobile suit, lined with *Thinsulate*. At the very coldest, I like the 4 in One Big Game parka made by Browning, of Route One, Morgan, Utah, 84050. This garment utilizes the layer principle, with an outer shell of Burlington 10 mile cloth laminated with waterproof *Gore-Tex*. The inner liner is insulated with DuPont *Thermolite*. Again, this outfit sports knitted wristlets and collar. There's a self-storing hood that rolls into the collar, and that comes in handy as an additional windbreak, but you'll still want the insulated cap with ear flaps under that parka hood. If you hunt in snow country, it is nice to have this parka in snow-white for camouflage reasons.

Speaking of snow camouflage, if you don't own a white parka, you might investigate your local paint store. Many paint stores sell an all white coverall intended for painters. They only cost a few bucks and if you buy the largest size, you can cover yourself and all your warm clothing with white—and do it for very little money. A hunter in a white coverall, lying on white snow, is almost invisible.

This well designed coverall by Columbia has many refinements, in the way of snug closures of wrists against cold and zipper legs to help donning over other clothing.

This hunter is using the snow camouflage parka made by Browning to hide from the sharp eyes of coyotes. It works equally well on patchy snow conditions for the goose hunter. Reversible, the other side is conventional brown camouflage.

When you have both snow and extreme cold to contend with, the warmest gear I've yet tested is produced for Browning. This consists of insulated bib overalls, big and roomy, and their storm parka with the liner. That liner is warm enough for most days, all alone. But when you "Velcro" it inside the insulated parka, both of which are *Gore-Tex* on the outside and *Thinsulate* on the inside, you can—literally—brave Antarctica without a worry.

This get-up provides three separate layers over the vital kidney and hip area, and you better believe it is warm. Because it is *Gore-Tex*, it breathes. During the dead of winter in our 9,000 foot country, I wore this over a wool shirt, light cotton underwear and a pair of wool pants, and stayed comfortable for eight hours in the biting wind and zero temperatures.

This outfit is a perfect example of the layering principle. You have many warm layers protecting your tender body, and you can remove them one at a time, as the day warms up, and stay comfortable all of the time.

Why remove layers? Your biggest enemy is moisture. If you sweat, and the sweat condenses on the inside of your insulating clothing, you are damp. When you are damp, you are cold—even inside the warmest of clothing.

Cotton is a lousy material to wear next to your skin. It gets wet quickly and it does a poor job of "wicking" moisture away from your body. Wool is the best of the natural fibers. It has the disadvantage of being itchy. We can forgive the itch if we remember that it retains some of its insulating qualities even when wet. Yes, wool is the best of the natural fibers, but it can't hold a candle to the un-natural fibers. Best of these is polypropylene. Now there is underwear made from polypropylene. It is the first layer. Wool should be the second, and *Gore-Tex* over *Thinsulate* should be the outer layer or layers.

Before leaving the subject of outer clothing, I want to go on record as saying that the new insulations are infinitely better than goose down. Sorry about that, fellows, but science has finally outdone the goose. Down insulation is wonderful when dry and not compressed. But it compresses easily, losing most of its insulating qualities. Wet, it is almost useless. *Thinsulate* and *Thermolite* and other synthetic insulators are infinitely better. They don't compress to any great extent and they are good insulators even when damp.

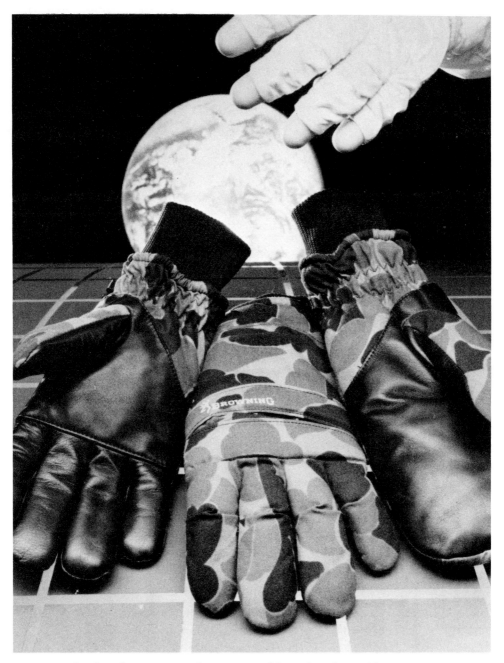

Keeping the hands warm is always a problem for the cold country goose hunter, but these new scientific materials used in Browning's mitts and gloves solve that problem.

Every experienced goose hunter knows that the worst place to get cold is on top of your head. Bareheaded goose hunters are obviously beginners, and I don't care if they grow enough for three men—human hair won't keep you from freezing the top of your head. I like a bill cap, because I want to shade my necessary eyeglasses so that they won't glint and give away my position to the alert goose. But the "seed cap" which is given away by the thousands all over farming country is not the answer. Those seed caps are usually well ventilated on the back half, and that we don't want. Billed caps are available from Browning, made of *Gore-Tex* and lined with flannel. If that isn't warm enough for your conditions, try Browning's new *Flap Cap*. Of *Gore-Tex*, lined with flannel, it also has ear flaps which can be lowered into place quickly, bringing nylon pile fluff to keep your ears warm. No matter which hunting headgear you choose, keep your head warm—for this is half the battle.

It is also hard to keep the finger of your shooting hand warm. For years I used a heavy mitten, with a slot cut through which I could stick the trigger finger. Trouble is that the slit let in the cold and the finger had a way of pushing itself out through the slot to be ready—long before there was any need to be ready. This made sure that my trigger finger was always frozen and considerably less than supple.

A better set up was the cotton jersey tight fitting glove, worn inside the loose fitting mitten. This kept the hand warm. When it was time to rise up and take your best shot, I put the mitten between my knees to pull it off and had a fairly warm shooting hand, encased in the light cloth glove, with which to fondle the trigger.

Developments during the past few years have provided us with much better hand coverings. Browning is in the forefront of this cold hands battle, offering two kinds of *Flexor* gloves (light and heavy) and a new Apollo "moon glove". The flexible *Flexor* gloves have additional insulation at the flex points to make sure that you don't squeeze the warmth out of it when squeezing Old Betsy in a death grip. At the same time, they let you "feel" the gun and shoot better. The mittens that go with this set are another matter entirely. I recommend them for the "very cold" situations which the exploring goose hunter will some- times encounter.

Feet are the last danger point. For my money, nothing can beat the oversize, very loose fitting, rubber-bottomed pac, lined with a roomy felt liner, over a bulky wool sock, which is over a thin wool sock. Most of us err on the side of fit. We fail to provide sufficient room inside the pacs for the big load we are going to put there. The felt liner must not be compressed, and the wool sock should not be compressed. Dead air space is a wonderful insulator, but not when the material is compressed enough to force out the dead air.

Nothing beats the warmth of the wool sock and felt liner combination, **when they are both dry.** Buy extra felt liners so that you can change them each day, giving the other pair a chance to dry out completely. The wool socks should be "high bulk" and cannot be too heavy. Sitting still is the real test of foot protection. I once sat for five hours in a cement blind, dynamited out of the granite alongside the St. Lawrence River in the beautiful province of Quebec. My feet were in two inches of water which was kept from freezing by my feet, I think. After the five hour wait, greater snow geese appeared on the northern horizon. My French speaking guide used only his vocal cords to call them in and we killed a limit. Ambient temperature was $-6°F$. Properly clothed, you can handle even those conditions. I shudder to think how I would have fared without the felt pacs, and without the insulated bib overalls from Browning, the down cap with ear flaps (down is okay in caps as long as it doesn't get either wet or compressed on your scalp), and the Apollo moon gloves.

It is a pious idea to keep your goose hunting gear separate from the rest of your outdoor wear. Save it strictly for the hunting blind. Used this way, you can amortize the cost of good gear over most of your lifetime, so don't skimp on the cost of clothes. Buy the best and you'll not be sorry. I am sure that there are many other manufacturers whose equipment is excellent. I've had experience with two top manufacturers' products—Columbia and Browning, and I can recommend their products for the goose hunter without blushing a bit.

Chapter 21

How to Cook Your Goose

A wild goose is a lean, trim, hard-bodied athlete. A wild goose is completely different from the fat, lazy, domestic goose. The most basic difference is that the wild goose is not full of lard. For this reason you must sauté everything that you intend to place inside a wild goose to be roasted. It will **NOT** cook itself in the goose grease, because there isn't any grease on this healthy bird's body.

Second basic difference is that you must baste more often, or cover the carcass completely with foil, to prevent it drying out. Outside of those two differences, it is routine to cook a wild goose. The flavor on the table is not routine.

Let's start with something completely different. How about a Louisiana style goose gumbo?

Goose Gumbo

Roast one whole goose of average size (5-8 pounds before cleaning). No need to stuff the goose, but baste it often or cook it in a bag to keep it from drying out. After it has cooled enough to work with, cut it up into one inch pieces—that's one inch cubed. Set aside.

Heat four tablespoons of bacon drippings, or cooking oil (bacon tastes better). Add 4 tablespoons of white flour and stir till smooth. Then add a couple of minced garlic cloves, four big chopped onions, 2 tablespoons of cayenne pepper, two bell peppers, chopped fine and two big sticks of celery, chopped fairly small. Stir this mess as it sautées, keep at it until the bell pepper and onions are soft. Then add 5 cups of chicken broth, 5 bay leaves, a pound of okra, chopped up; 1 big can of tomatoes (don't bother to drain it) and a small can of tomato paste. Simmer this concoction for 15 minutes.

Then add the chopped goose and let the whole works simmer slowly for an hour or two, stirring occasionally to make sure it doesn't stick and burn. For the more daring palate, add a dash or two of tabasco, or a heaping teaspoonful of "file gumbo", the real thing—no imitations, please.

Roast Young Goose

For tender young geese, you'll need
One lemon
One apple sized onion, chopped to half inch size pieces
One cup of chopped apple, green or ripe.
Half a cup of margarine, not diet margarine which burns instead of melting.
One cup of chopped dried apricots.
Two handfuls of croutons—not sage or garlic, just plain croutons.
Four slices of bacon.
Quarter the lemon and use it to rub the bird inside and out. Squeeze it to get out the remaining juice and put that juice in the body cavity. Sauté the onion in margarine till soft, then add the other ingredients, all mixed together. Salt and pepper to taste. Stuff the bird, and sew the opening shut. Skewer the strips of bacon to the outside of the

breast. Place bird, breast side up, in a brown paper bag and lay in roasting pan. Set oven at 325°, allow thirty minutes per pound of raw goose—weighed before you stuff it, of course.

Fruit Stuffed Goose

Mix together:
3 and one half cups of soft bread cubes
One and one half cup of diced apple
Two oranges, sectioned
Half cup of raisins
3/4 cup of chopped onion
One cup of grapes, halved
One cup of melted butter or oleo

Mix the whole works thoroughly and stuff the bird with it. Sew shut and skewer bacon strips on outside of breast as in previous recipe. Good!

Twice Stuffed Goose

This is my personal favorite. It works equally well with young or adult geese. Get all the pinfeathers and fuzz off (try singeing them off with a fire built of rolled up newspaper, but do it outside!). Then soak at least four hours in a bath of lightly salted cold water to draw out dried or clotted blood. Then rinse the bird thoroughly under running cold water to remove excess salt.

Next you'll need a lot of goodies:
3 fist-sized onions
2 cans of chopped mushroom bits and pieces
2 cups of ripe olives, pitted
2 packages of "brown and long-grained" rice
3 cans of cream of mushroom soup (do not dilute)
One small can of diced pimentoes.

Ready? Sauté the onions in butter. When soft, add the olives and the mushrooms. Simmer all together. Next boil the rice, including the flavoring package which comes with it. Boil almost all of the water away and set it aside to cool.

Next, spoon all of the sautéed ingredients into the wild rice, stirring well. Shove all of this into the body cavity of the goose, and lay the excess around the goose and piled on top of the goose.

Roast your goose in a preheated oven at 350° for one hour. Then turn the oven down to 300° and let it cook slowly for several hours. When a fork slides in easily, remove the bird from oven and scoop out all of the body cavity stuffing. Mix it thoroughly with the excess which lies in the bottom of the roasting pan. Stir well. Now comes the different part.

Mix the rest of the stuffing material with the cream of mushroom soup. Do not dilute the soup; we want it thick and gooey. Pile this mixture an inch thick atop the goose's breast. Return the goose to the oven, uncovered, and cook till very tender. Distribute the pimento on top of the goose for visual appeal.

The dressing so created is almost as good as the goose. There's no gravy—but you won't mind.

Whitefronted Goose Special

A young whitefront is the finest eating there is. To prove it, you'll need a goose, plus:

Half a lemon

Glaze ingredients, consisting of half a cup of peach marmalade, chopped ginger, three cups of ginger preserves, three tablespoons of cooking sherry, half a cup of honey, all stirred together.

One large onion, chopped

Six strips of bacon

Rub the lemon all over the goose, putting excess juice inside. Then sprinkle the chopped onion inside the young whitefront. Baste the outside of the goose carefully with the glaze mixture. Make sure it is well covered. Pop it into a broiler for 15 minutes to set the glaze. Then baste it again, very carefully. Drape the onion strips over the breast and put it back in a 325° degree oven until tender to the fork. Baste occasionally with the remaining glaze. Serve it hot and smile!

How to Soften up a Tough old Goose

This time I want you to skin the goose. I hate to, but this time we are doing radical things to save a tough old goose for the epicures table. Put the naked carcass to soak in lightly salted cold weater. Then get together the following:

1 clove of garlic, sliced in half
1 big onion, diced
3 big sprigs of fresh parsley
1 cup of port, burgundy or sherry, just so long as it is red
A teaspoon of Worcestershire sauce
Two cans Cream of Mushroom soup
1 can whole mushrooms, drained
1 and one half cups sour cream
Lots of melted butter

Drain and dry the goose, rub inside and out with the garlic clove. Toss out the garlic. Put the bird in crockpot or slow cooker, sprinkle onion and parsley over its breast. Pour on the wine and Worcestershire. Cover it with the mushrooms and mushroom soup and stir well. Cover and slow cook for eight hours. Now you have a goose that falls off its bones. Good. Remove the boneless goose to a bowl and carefully and slowly add the sour cream to the fluid mixture, being careful not to let the sour cream form chunks.

Put goose meat in an individual serving bowl. Pour the sour cream mixture over the top, add a dollop of butter on top of everything and put it on the table.

Leftovers?

We usually don't leave anything the first time, but if you have left over goose, it makes up into excellent goose soup or goose salad. Chunk the cold goose meat and add it to any fresh vegetable or fresh fruit salad, with your favorite dressing. Try it!

London-Broiled Goose

The next time you get lucky and bring home a limit of snows, try this one. After the cleaned bird has soaked overnight in lightly salted water, take a very sharp knife and slice off strips of breast meat—pieces about half an inch thick. You won't get too many from each goose. Marinate the slices of raw goose meat overnight in a mixture made up of:

A half cup of vinegar, a crushed clove of garlic, two tablespoons of Worcestershire sauce, a dozen peppercorns (bruised or mashed), a couple of bay leaves, and a careful dash of *Tabasco* sauce. Add enough cold water to allow marinade to cover the meat.

Ready? Wipe each piece dry on paper towelling, and cook quickly over the grill. Sear the outsides to hold in the juices, and leave the inside slightly pink. They'll come back for more.

By the way, don't waste the rest of that goose. It has the makings of an excellent goose soup.

Roast Goose with Sauerkraut

You'll need three pounds of sauerkraut for the average sized goose. If you've got one of the "maximas" make it six pounds of sauerkraut and invite your friends. Drain and rinse the salt off the sauerkraut. Sauté a couple of big onions in bacon drippings, sauté until all soft and transparent, but not browned. Add the sauerkraut to the onions and then add two cups of diced apples, two cups of raw potato, sliced thin (we use a colander). Salt and pepper to taste, including salting the inside of the goose.

Stuff the goose with the sauerkraut, onions, apples and potatoes mixture. Sew him up tight and roast as usual, preferably in a brown bag or under a tinfoil tent.

Potato and Sausage-Stuffed Goose

This is a variation on the sauerkraut theme, without the kraut. Use a pound of sausage, well-browned in your frying pan. Then sauté the giblets in the sausage drippings; add two cups of chopped onions, two cups of bread crumbs (more if the goose is large) and a couple of eggs well stirred. Blend all of this with three cups of mashed potatoes. Use it all to stuff your goose.

Photo Credits

Front Matter– Photograph by Frank R. Martin
(p.11)– Photograph by the author
(p.14)– Photograph by Frank R. Martin
(p.15)– Photograph by Frank R. Martin
(p.17)– Photograph by Frank R. Martin
(p.19)– Photograph by the author
(p.21)– Photograph by the author
(p.23)– Photograph by Judd Cooney
(p.25)– Photograph by the author
(p.27)– Photograph by the author
(p.28)– Photograph by Judd Cooney
(p.29)– Photograph by Judd Cooney
(p.30)– Photograph by the author
(p.32)– Photograph by Ed Bry
(p.34)– Photograph by the author
(p.36)– Photograph by the author
(p.41)– Photograph by Joel Arrington
(p.42)– Photograph by Joel Arrington
(p.43)– Photograph by Joel Arrington
(p.44)– Photograph by Luther Partin
(p.45)– Photograph by the author
(p.51)– Photograph by Wilf Pyle
(p.52)– Photograph by Wilf Pyle
(p.53)– Photograph by Wilf Pyle
(p.54)– Photograph by Wilf Pyle
(p.57)– Photograph by Frank Martin
(p.76)– Photograph by the author
(p.83)– Photograph by the author
(p.89)– Photograph by the author
(p.93)– Photograph by Bill Perry
(p.95)– Photograph by Ed Bry
(p.96)– Photograph by Ed Bry

(p.97)– Photograph by the author
(p.99)– Photographs by the author
(p.100)– Photograph by the author
(p.102)– Photograph by Jack Dermid, N.C. Wildlife Resources Commission
(p.106)– Photograph by L.A. Wilkie
(p.112)– Photograph by the author
(p.115)– Photograph by Frank Heidelbauer
(p.116)– Photograph by the author
(p.120)– Photograph by the author
(p.121)– Photograph by L.A. Wilkie
(p.123)– Photograph by Bill Perry (top)
(p.123)– Photograph by Joel Arrington (bottom)
(p.130)– Photograph by the Missouri Conservation Commission
(p.138)– Photograph by Christopher Batin
(p.140)– Photograph by Christopher Batin
(p.145)– Photograph by Christopher Batin
(p.153)– Photograph by Ed Dentry
(p.154)– Photograph by Ed Dentry
(p.154)– Photograph by Ed Dentry
(p.158)– Drawing by Bob Hines
(p.159)– Drawing by Bob Hines
(p.160)– Drawing by Bob Hines
(p.161)– Drawing by Bob Hines
(p.162)– Photograph by Rex Gary Schmidt
(p.163)– Photograph by Earl Craven
(p.165)– Photograph by the author
(p.168)– Photograph by Frank R. Martin
(p.169)– Photograph by Frank R. Martin
(p.170)– Photograph by the author
(p.173)– Photograph by Frank R. Martin
(p.178)– Photograph by Ed Bry
(p.179)– Photograph by Judd Cooney
(p.181)– Photograph by the author
(p.183)– Photograph by the author
(p.198)– Photograph by Frank Heidelbauer
(p.204)– Photograph by the author
(p.206)– Photograph by Ed Bry
(p.208)– Photograph by the author
(p.209)– Photograph by the author